Praise for J ˓

The Pirates of Somalia

"A first-of-its kind book. . . . Takes readers through the evolution of the pirate groups from garrulous, self-proclaimed vigilantes who claim they are protecting Somalia's waters from illegal fishing vessels to the deadly criminal gangs they are today."

—Associated Press

"Convincing. . . . In Bahadur's telling, the fractured, tribal governance of Somalia's territories is almost unbelievable in its dysfunction. And the year-by-year evolution of Somalian piracy is mesmerizing. . . . Look to *The Pirates of Somalia* for an aggregation of all the news stories about this phenomenon over the past four years, with the additional, intimate layer—stories of the pirates from the pirates themselves—that no one else was reckless enough to get."

—*The Plain Dealer*

"This vivid and intelligent study of Somali pirates uncovers the reckless men behind the nation's most lucrative business. . . . A balanced and fascinating portrait." —*The Sunday Times* (London)

"An insightful report. . . . Revelatory journalism and astute analysis of causes and solutions that prove far more informative than any TV footage about the contemporary piracy problem." —*Booklist*

"An engaging account, full of solid analysis. . . . What's especially impressive (aside from Bahadur's sheer nerve in insinuating himself among these dangerous men in a lawless corner of the world) is the amassing of multiple perspectives—of pirates and policymakers—that support a rich, suspenseful account." —*Publishers Weekly*

JAY BAHADUR

The Pirates of Somalia

Jay Bahadur's articles have appeared in *The Times* (London), *The New York Times*, the *Financial Times*, and *The Globe and Mail* (Toronto). He has advised the U.S. government and has worked as a freelance correspondent for CBS News. Bahadur currently lives in Nairobi.

www.jaybahadur.com
Twitter: @PuntlandPirates

The Pirates of Somalia

INSIDE THEIR HIDDEN WORLD

JAY BAHADUR

VINTAGE BOOKS
A Division of Random House, Inc.
New York

FIRST VINTAGE BOOKS EDITION, AUGUST 2012

The Library of Congress has cataloged the Pantheon edition as follows:
Bahadur, Jay.
The pirates of Somalia : inside their hidden world / Jay Bahadur.
p. cm.
Includes bibliographical references and index.
1. Pirates—Somalia—21st century.
2. Piracy—Somalia—21st century.
3. Hijacking of ships—Somalia—21st century.
4. Puntland (Somalia)—Economic conditions.
5. Somalia—Politics and government—1991-
6. Bahadur, Jay—Travel—Somalia—Puntland. I. Title.
DT403.2.B34 2011
364.164096773—dc22
2011011731

Vintage ISBN: 978-0-307-47656-2

Author photograph © David G. Christen
Maps on pages vii and viii by Susan MacGregor/Digital Zone

www.vintagebooks.com

Printed in the United States of America
10 9 8 7 6 5 4 3 2 1

*To Ali, without whose infectious love for Africa
this book would not exist*

Contents

Somalia

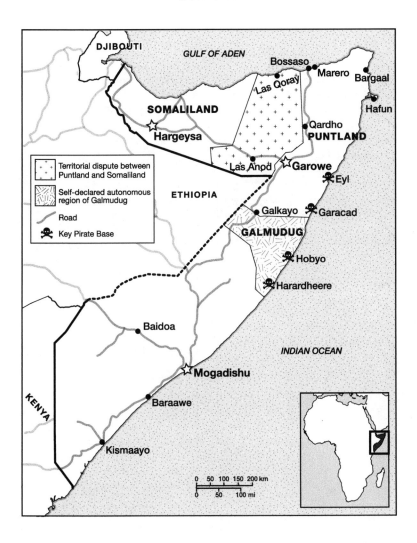

Expansion of Pirate Operations

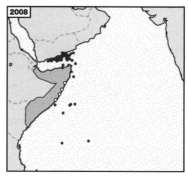

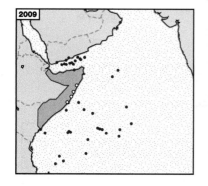

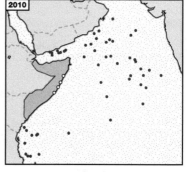

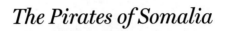

The Pirates of Somalia

Prologue

Where the White Man Runs Away

IT WAS MY FIRST TRIP TO AFRICA.

I arrived in Somalia in the frayed seat of a 1970s Soviet Antonov propeller plane, heading into the internationally unrecognized region of Puntland on a solo quest to meet some present-day pirates. The 737s of Dubai, with their meal services and functioning seatbelts, were a distant memory; the plane I was in was not even allowed to land in Dubai, and the same probably went for the unkempt, ill-tempered Ukrainian pilot.

To the ancient Egyptians, Punt had been a land of munificent treasures and bountiful wealth; in present times, it was a land of people who robbed wealth from the rest of the world. Modern Puntland, a self-governing region in northeastern Somalia, may or may not be the successor to the Punt of ancient times, but I was soon to discover that it contained none of the gold and ebony that dazzled the Egyptians—save perhaps for the colours of the sand and the skin of the nomadic goat and camel herders who had inhabited it for centuries.

The cabin absorbed the heat of the midday African sun like a Dutch oven, thickening the air until it was unbearable to breathe. Sweat poured freely off my skin and soaked into the torn cloth of my seat cover. Male passengers fanned themselves with the Russian-language aircraft safety cards; the women fanned their children. The high whine of the Antonov's propellers changed pitch as it accelerated along the Djibouti runway, building towards a droning crescendo that I had not heard outside of decades-old movies.

The stories I had heard of these planes did nothing to put me at ease: a vodka-soaked technician banging on exposed engine parts with a wrench; a few months prior, a plant-nosed landing at Bossaso airstrip after a front landing strut had refused to extend. Later, in Bossaso, I saw the grounded craft, abandoned where it had crashed, a few lackadaisical guards posted nearby to prevent people from stripping the valuable metal.

This flight was like a forgotten relic of the Cold War, a physical testament to long-defunct Somali-Soviet geopolitical ties that had disintegrated with the countries themselves; its Ukrainian crew, indentured servants condemned forever to ferry passengers along this neglected route.

Over the comm system, the Somali steward offered a prayer in triplicate: *Allahu akbar, Allahu akbar, Allahu akbar,* as the plane gained speed. The whine heightened to a mosquito-like buzz and we left the ground behind, setting an eastward course for Somalia, roughly shadowing the Gulf of Aden coastline.

* * *

As I approached my thirty-fifth weary hour of travel, my desire to socialize with fellow passengers had diminished, but on purely self-serving grounds I forced myself to chat eagerly with anyone throwing a curious glance in my direction. I had never met my Somali host, Mohamad Farole, and any friend I made on the plane was a potential roof over my head if my ride didn't show. Remaining alone at the landing strip was not an option; news travels around Somalia as fast as the ubiquitous cellphone towers are able to transmit it, and a lone white man bumming around the airstrip would be public knowledge sooner than I cared to contemplate.

When he learned that I was travelling to Garowe, Puntland's capital city, the bearded man sitting next to me launched into the unfortunate tale of the last foreigner he knew to make a similar voyage: a few months previous, a Korean man claiming to be a Muslim had turned up in the capital, alone and unannounced. Not speaking a word of Somali, he nonetheless succeeded in finding a residence and beginning a life in his unusual choice of adoptive homeland.

He lasted almost two weeks. On his twelfth day in Puntland, a group of rifle-toting gunmen accosted the man in broad daylight as he strolled unarmed through the streets. Rather than let himself be taken hostage, the Korean made a fight of it, managing to struggle free and run. He made it several metres before one of his bemused would-be captors casually shot him in the leg. The shot set off a hue and cry, and in the ensuing clamour the gunmen dispersed and someone helped the man reach a medical clinic. I later learned from another source that he was a fugitive, on the run from the Korean authorities. His thought process, I could only assume, was that Somalia was the last place on earth that his government would look for him. He was probably right.

* * *

Just a few months earlier, I had been a recent university graduate, killing the days writing tedious reports for a market research firm in Chicago, and trying to break into journalism with the occasional cold pitch to an unresponsive editor. I had no interest in journalism school, which I thought of as a waste of two of the best years of my life—years that I should spend in the fray, learning how to do my would-be job in places where no one else would go.

Somalia was a good candidate, jockeying with Iraq and Afghanistan for the title of the most dangerous country in the world. The country had commanded a soft spot in my heart since my PoliSci days, when I had wistfully dreamt of bringing the astounding democratic success of the tiny self-declared Republic of Somaliland (Puntland's western neighbour) to the world's attention.

The headline-grabbing hijacking of the tank transport MV *Faina* in September 2008 presented me with a more realistic opportunity. I sent out some feelers to a few Somali news services, and within ten minutes had received an enthusiastic response from Radio Garowe, the lone news outlet in Puntland's capital city. After a few long emails and a few short phone calls with Radio Garowe's founder, Mohamad Farole, I decided to buy a ticket to Somalia.

It took multiple tickets, as it turned out. Getting to Somalia was an aerophobe's nightmare—a forty-five-hour voyage that took me through Frankfurt, Dubai, Djibouti, Bossaso, and finally Galkayo. In Dubai, I joined the crowd of diaspora Somalis, most making short visits to see their families, pushing cart upon cart overflowing with goods from the outside world. Curious eyes began to glance my way, scanning, no doubt, for signs of mental instability. I was in no position to help them make the diagnosis; by the first leg of my trip, I had already lost the ability to judge objectively whether what I was doing was sane or not. News reports of the numerous journalists kidnapped in Puntland fixated my imagination. I channelled the hours of nervous energy into studying the lone Somali language book I had been able to dig up at the public library; I scribbled answers to exercises into my notebook with an odd sense of urgency, as if cramming for an exam that would take place as soon as I set foot in Somalia.

The last white face disappeared at Djibouti's dilapidated, near-deserted airport, as American F-16s performed eardrum-shattering training manoeuvres overhead. By the time the plane landed in Galkayo, I was the only non-Somali passenger on board.

* * *

The Antonov's first stop was Bossaso, Puntland's northernmost port and most populous city. We wove back and forth over water and land, as Somalia's undulating coastline cut back and forth across the vector of our flight. Out of the scratched porthole, the solid azure of the Gulf of Aden below was broken only by intermittent white cracks marking the location of swells; from the sky, they looked like fissures erupting on the surface of a perfectly smooth blue rock face. As the plane swung back towards the coast, the lines of white increased in number, joined by the occasional fishing trawler cutting its own independent trail across the water.

As we crossed over land, Bossaso came into view. It was the first sign of life Somalia had displayed, a settlement rising out of the vast, lunar wasteland enveloping it. From the air, the city appeared as a clutter of corrugated roof buildings, gathering in a concentrated burst before spilling into the sea. The minarets of occasional mosques poked out of the conglomeration of one- and two-storey structures. A miniature range of denuded mountains, looking like cropped volcanoes, formed a crescent around the city.

The plane banked precipitously and began its descent towards the thin stretch of unclaimed beach lying between city and ocean, in which Bossaso airstrip was nestled. The temperature in the cabin began to rise once more as the Antonov left the higher altitudes. Within a few minutes, the plane had come to a bumping stop on the sand-coated runway.

The thought hit me for the first time: *I am in fucking Somalia.*

Somalia is like a country out of a twisted fairy tale, an ethereal land given substance only by the stories we are told of it. Everything known by the outside world has been constructed from news reports spilling out of the country over the last twenty years: warlords, famine, Black Hawks, jihadis, and now pirates. Along with bananas and livestock, international news is one of the few items that Somalia can still claim to export, and crossing the border from Djibouti into Somalia had brought me from the world of news consumers into the world of news producers.

The stopover was brief; as soon as the Antonov had finished refuelling, the remaining passengers climbed back on board and it took off once more, setting a course for Galkayo, a city straddling Puntland's southern border. The desert below stretched in shades of brown and blond; evaporated riverbeds scarred the pockmarked terrain, carving valleys in their wake. Galkayo is a dangerous place, a crucible where the northern Darod and the southern Hawiye clan families meet, cleaving the city along its east–west axis; the reputed English translation of the city's name, "where the white man runs away," did not put me at ease. Though I had initially assumed that the site marked a decisive victory by Somali independence fighters over British or Italian colonial forces, I later discovered that Galkayo was the location of a much earlier battle between invading Somalis and the non-Muslim indigenous inhabitants.

After another ninety minutes and seven hundred kilometres, Galkayo appeared. We touched down on another dusty landing strip, tires churning to a stop near an expectant crowd. It was the end of the line. I stepped once more down the six shaky steps onto Somali soil, and looked anxiously through the milling throng.

My own name had never sounded as sweet as when I heard it being called from across the landing strip. The voice belonged to Mohamad's cousin Abdirizak, who waved and walked hurriedly towards me. He was short and trim, with a joyous laugh, warm smile, and a receding hairline. Hours of pent-up stress drained out of my body.

Abdi and I proceeded to a customs office, a largely empty building containing a few uniformed officials milling around behind bare wood and glass partitions. One of the bored agents looked me over and demanded twenty dollars for an "airport tax" and another twenty dollars for a visa, which he impressed onto my passport with a stamp that looked to be left over from the days of the collapsed Somali Republic.[1] Asking how long I wished to remain in the country, he scribbled my answer into the allotted field on the still-drying stamp—apparently the twenty-dollar visa was a flat rate.

Abdi led me to a gleaming white-and-chrome Land Cruiser. Perched at either end of the back seat were two UN-trained bodyguards, Said and Abdirashid, who would accompany me like another heartbeat for the next six weeks. They cradled their worn AK-47s between the pant legs of their beige uniforms; crudely sewn on their sleeves were patches with the letters "SPU"—Special Police Unit—superimposed on a blue stag's head, the emblem of the Puntland police.

In Somalia, 4x4s are needed to get around even in urban areas; with the exception of the main thoroughfare, Galkayo's unpaved streets were worn down to their bare bones, the dirt eaten away by tire treads to the uneven rock beneath. The surfaces of the buildings, some whitewashed, some matching the dull brown of the road, were chipped and worn, and occasionally bullet-marked. The more upscale houses were covered with geometric patterns of vibrant blues, greens, and yellows, like the colours of a Van Gogh canvas. Similarly vivid paintings on the facades of shops—bags of flour, cans of oil, generic bottles of pills—advertised what was sold within. The Land Cruiser rocked to a stop in front of one of these; the listing English letters above the entrance read "General Store," and one of the SPU guards dashed inside and returned with some cream-filled biscuits and a number of bottles of water. In the mid-afternoon heat, the streets were largely deserted except for a few children, who skipped around me cautiously.

The one-lane highway connecting Galkayo to Garowe and Bossaso is the sole road running through Puntland along its north–south axis, a solitary link stretching across seven hundred kilometres of desert. Its decrepit state was symbolic of the neglect the region experienced under former dictator Siad Barre, and from the international community more recently. The three-decade-old Chinese concrete was crumbling and corroded, and craterous potholes turned the 250-kilometre journey from Galkayo to Garowe into a four- or five-hour jolting ordeal. It was January 2009, the onset of the first of Puntland's two dry seasons, the *jiilaal*, and parched shrubs dotted the barren landscape; the dust clung to my skin until my shirt felt like fine sandpaper. Piles of bottles, old tires, and the odd stripped chassis lined both sides of the road; discarded plastic bags, struggling in the clutches of spiny bushes, waved at us spasmodically as we drove by. Every so often an impassive camel plodded across the road, slowing us to a near halt.

At irregular intervals, buildings of thatched branches and the occasional panel of corrugated metal clustered into settlements by the side of the highway. The boundaries of these shantytowns were marked by speed bumps built by the inhabitants out of packed dirt and rocks. A few empty gasoline drums blocked the road at the entrance to each village, with two or three listless guards loitering around the makeshift checkpoints.

At one of these pit stops we abruptly turned off the road and pulled into an open-air restaurant, its plastic tables and chairs almost spilling onto the highway. A few words were exchanged, and out came metal plates heaped with sticky rice sopped in goat's milk, flanked by fist-sized chunks of gristly camel meat. My two guards, sharing one of the plates, used their hands to squish the rice into pasty balls, which they proceeded to deposit into their mouths. I decided to use the spoon that had been offered to me, feeling some- how like an elitist in doing so. They looked attentively at me and smiled, waiting for my reaction to tasting camel meat for the first time. I picked at the stringy meat with a knife and my teeth as best I could, smiling back vacuously.

As we ate, a menacing semicircle of youth gradually formed around me, glowering eyes filled with mistrust and suspicion. I tried to lean as casually as possible against the back of my plastic lawn chair, but I was grateful for the SPU.

Four hours down the road, darkness fell. Close to the equator, night arrives startlingly quickly, with dusk relegated to the role of minor broker between night and day. The straight track ahead dis- solved into the night beyond the reach of our high beams. No other cars were on the road, and the blackness around us was absolute. We climbed over the last in a series of gentle hills, and the muffled lights of Garowe finally came into view.

Soon we passed a checkpoint where a few yawning soldiers in fatigues hurriedly waved us through, then an abandoned gas sta- tion, the UN compound, and many other buildings I was unable to make out. Under the city's muted street lights, Garowe was reduced to a monochromatic grey. Partway through the city we pulled off the main road and struck out onto Garowe's pitch-black streets. Our headlights began to reveal haphazard piles of stone littered around spacious plots of empty land, evidence of Garowe's ongoing building boom. We hit another, miniature, checkpoint, nothing more than a log laid across the path, where a uniformed soldier shouted at us to extinguish our headlights, glanced inside the car, and waved us through.

More soldiers were lounging around the entrance to Mohamad's house. Our driver honked, causing a handful of them to jump to attention and rush to swing open the spiked iron gate. It was past nine o'clock, but multiple Land Cruisers were parked in the driveway and the courtyard was still bustling with activity. Until the last few days, the newly elected president of Puntland had lived here, before moving into the official residence inside the government compound.

I was sleepily ushered through the house and into its only functioning office, where Mohamad sat behind a desk covered by stacks of paper and a laptop. His frame, short and stocky, was the antithesis of the lanky and imperious figure that typified most Somalis. In the pale-green hue cast by the room's only light source, I could not make out the details of his face, not that it made a difference; I had never so much as seen a photograph of the man who was to protect me for the next month and a half. We shook hands and exchanged quick pleasantries.

Soon Abdi and I were back in the dark meandering city corridors, twisting down nameless streets where I saw nothing and remembered nothing, and pulled to a stop in front of a modest-sized residence with a blue gate. We passed through a courtyard and past a set of swinging metal doors into the house. As the SPU set up camp in the courtyard, Abdi showed me down a hall to my room. I tossed down the sports bag carrying my computer, notebooks, and malaria medication next to the bed.

I had scarcely pulled the mosquito netting over the bed before I was asleep.

* * *

I was to spend the next six weeks living in Garowe, a rapidly expanding city at the very heart of the pirates' tribal homeland. My local partner, Mohamad, was the son of the newly elected president, Abdirahman Farole, a fact that made me privy to backroom political dealings, stories, gossip, and daily impressions of life that went beyond the perceptions of reporters flying in to take snapshots of the gang behind the latest tanker hijacking. During this first trip to Puntland, I was shocked to encounter no other foreigners until my final day in the country, when, long-bearded and bedraggled, I briefly met with an Australian television crew hours before flying out of Bossaso. For an outsider, my access to the region was truly unique.

Contrary to the oft-recycled one-liners found in most news reports, Somalia is not a country in anarchy. Indeed, to even speak of Somalia as a uniform entity is a mischaracterization, because in the wake of the civil war the country has broken down into a number of autonomous enclaves. Founded in 1998 as a tribal sanctuary for the hundreds of thousands of Darod clanspeople fleeing massacres in the south, Puntland State of Somalia comprises approximately 1.3 million people, one-quarter to one-third of Somalia's total land mass (depending on whom you talk to), and almost half of its coastline. Straddling the shipping bottleneck of the Gulf of Aden and the Indian Ocean, it was the natural candidate to become the epicentre of the recent outbreak of Somali piracy.

In writing this book, I had the difficult task of bringing a fresh perspective to a topic that continues to inundate the pages of news publications around the world. Pirates make good copy: there is something about them that animates the romantic imagination. But reports of daring hijackings in the international section of the newspaper are the print equivalents of the talking heads on the evening news; their polarizing effect may attract people to an issue, but they do not tell the whole story. Descriptions of hijackings are a black-and-white sketch that I intend to render in colour.

The Pirates of Somalia is about the pirates' lives both inside and outside of attack skiffs: how they spend their money, their houses, the clothes they wear, the cars they drive, the women they consort with, their drug of choice—in short, what makes them human beings, not simply the AK-47-toting thugs who appear in feature articles. Of course, this book is also about what they *do*—the occupation that has made them the scourge of every major seafaring nation. Over the course of my two visits to Puntland, from January to March and June to July of 2009—as well as subsequent trips to London, Romania, Nairobi, and Mombasa—I spoke not only to pirates, but also to government officials, former hostages, scholars, soldiers, and jailors. Through this panorama of perspectives, I hope to tell the full story of the most nefarious of modern-day buccaneers—the pirates of Puntland.

1

Boyah

BOYAH IS A PIRATE.

He was one of the "old boys," an original pirate, quietly pursuing his trade in the waters of his coastal hometown of Eyl years before it galvanized the world's imagination as an infamous pirate haven in mid-2008. Abdullahi Abshir, known as Boyah—who claimed to have hijacked more than twenty-five ships—looked down on the recent poseurs, the headline-grabbers who had bathed in the international media spotlight, and it showed; he exuded a self-assured superiority.

It had taken five days to arrange this meeting. Pirates are hard to track down, constantly moving around and changing phone numbers, and are generally not reachable before twelve or one in the afternoon. Days earlier, frustrated and eager to begin interviewing, I had naively suggested approaching some suspected pirates on the streets of Garowe. Habitually munching on narcotic leaves of khat, they are easy enough to spot, their gleaming Toyota four-wheel-drives slicing paths around beaten-up wheelbarrows and pushcarts on Garowe's eroded streets. My Somali hosts laughed derisively, explaining that to do so would invite kidnapping, robbery, or, at the very least, unwanted surveillance. In Somalia, everything is done through connections, be they clan, family, or friend, and these networks are expansive and interminable; you have to *know* one another, and it seems sometimes that everyone does. Warsame,[1] my guide and interpreter, had been on and off the phone for the better part of a week, attempting to coax his personal network into producing Boyah. Eventually it responded, and Boyah presented himself.

I was being taken to a mutually agreed meeting place in the passenger side of an aging white station wagon, cruising out of Garowe on the city's sole paved road. Along this stretch, the concrete had endured remarkably well, with few of the jarring potholes that routinely force cars onto the shoulder from Garowe to Galkayo. Said and Abdirashid perched attentively in the back seat, and in the rear-view mirror was a sleek new Land Cruiser, a shining symbol of the recent money pouring into Garowe. It carried Boyah, Colonel Omar Abdullahi Farole (the cousin of my host Mohamad Farole), and Warsame. Other than our two vehicles, the road was empty, stretching unencumbered through a stony desert dotted with greenish shrubs. The thought that I was being taken to be executed in a deserted field—the unfortunate product of the BBC's Africa news section and too many Las Vegas mob movies—rattled around in my head for a few seconds.

We arrived at our destination, a virtually abandoned roadside farm fifteen kilometres outside of Garowe. Boyah had recently contracted tuberculosis, and Warsame insisted that we meet him in an open space. As we stepped out of our respective vehicles, I caught my first glimpse of Boyah. He looked to be in his early forties, immensely tall and with an air of menace about him; the brief, calculating glance with which he scanned me left the distinct impression that he was capable of chatting amiably or robbing me with the same equanimity. He was wearing a *ma'awis*, a traditional sarong-like robe of a clan elder, and an *imaamad*, a decorative shawl, was slung over his left shoulder. On his feet was a pair of spit-shined ebony leather sandals.

Boyah turned immediately and loped down the dirt path leading towards the farm, Colonel Omar following paces behind him. Threading his way through the mishmash of tomato plants and lemon trees that constituted this eclectic farm, Boyah wove back and forth along the path, like a bird looking for a roosting spot. Finally, he settled on a site in a cool, shady clearing, where an overhead thatching of branches had created an almost cave-like atmosphere. He squatted in the centre of the clearing and began to toy with a *dhiil*—a wooden vat used by nomads to store milk—that someone had left on top of a nearby stack of wood. His mobile phone resting in his right hand, Boyah remained singularly focused on the oblong container in front of him, twirling it on the hardened dirt like a solo game of spin-the-bottle.

Other than the farm's owner and his wife, no one was remotely close by, yet the Special Police Unit officers took up positions at either ends of the clearing with an amusing military officiousness. The meeting place filled with the rest of our party, and I decided it was time to force Boyah to acknowledge my presence. I walked up to him and greeted him with the standard *Salaam álaykum,* and was not surprised when Boyah and those around him responded with startled laughter before quickly offering the formulaic response: *Álaykum salaam.* Somalis were routinely astonished when I demonstrated the slightest knowledge of their culture or language—even a phrase that they shared with the entire Islamic world.

We seated ourselves on some nearby logs and I began the interview. As I forced out my first question through Warsame, I hesitated to use the word "pirate" to describe Boyah. The closest Somali translation of the word is *burcad badeed,* which literally means "ocean robber," a political statement I was anxious to avoid. In much the same way that revolutionaries straddle the semantic fence separating "freedom fighters" from "terrorists," Boyah and his brothers-in-arms did not like to call themselves "pirates" in their native tongue. In an alliterative display of defiance, they referred to themselves as *badaadinta badah,* "saviours of the sea," a term that is most often translated in the English-speaking media as "coast guard." Boyah joked that he was the "chief of the coast guard," a title he invoked with pride. To him, his actions had been in protection of *his* sea, the native waters he had known his whole life; his hijackings, a legitimate form of taxation levied *in absentia* on behalf of a defunct government that he represented in spirit, if not in law.

His story was typical of many coastal dwellers who had turned to piracy since the onset of the civil war almost twenty years ago. In 1994, he still worked as an artisanal lobster diver in Eyl—"one of the best," he said. Looking at his rakish figure, I believed him; it was easy to imagine his lanky form navigating the deepest oceanic crags in the reefs below. Since then, the lobster population off the coast of Eyl has been devastated by foreign fishing fleets—mostly Chinese, Taiwanese, and Korean ships, Boyah said. Using steel-pronged drag fishing nets, these foreign trawlers did not bother with nimble explorations of the reefs: they uprooted them, netting the future livelihood of the nearby coastal people along with the day's catch. Through their rapacious destruction of the reefs, foreign drag-fishers wiped out the lobster breeding grounds. Today, according to Boyah, there are no more lobsters to be found in the waters off Eyl.[2]

So he began to fish a different species, lashing out at those who could out-compete him on the ocean floor, but who were no match for him on its surface. From 1995 to 1997, Boyah and others captured three foreign fishing vessels, keeping the catch and ransoming the crew. By 1997, the foreign fishing fleets had become more challenging prey, entering into protection contracts with local warlords that made armed guards and anti-aircraft guns regular fixtures on the decks of their ships. So, like all successful hunters, Boyah and his men adapted to their changing environment, and began going after commercial shipping vessels. They soon attracted others to their cause.

"There are about five hundred pirates operating around Eyl. I am their chairman," he said, claiming to head up a "Central Committee" composed of the bosses of thirty-five other groups. The position of chairman, however, did not imbue Boyah with the autocratic powers of a traditional gang leader. Rather, Eyl's pirate groups functioned as a kind of loose confederation, in which Boyah was a key organizer, recruiter, financier, and mission commander. But would-be applicants for the position of pirate (Eyl Division) had to come to him, he claimed. The interview was not too gruelling—Boyah's sole criteria for a recruit were that he own a gun and be "a hero, and accept death"—qualities that grace the CVs of many desperate local youth. Turnover in Boyah's core group was low; when I asked if his men ever used their new-found wealth to leave Somalia, he laughed and shook his head.

"The only way they leave is when they die." He smiled and added offhandedly that a member of his band had departed the previous night, dying in his sleep of undisclosed reasons. "You were supposed to meet him," Boyah told me.

What makes for an attractive target? I asked. Boyah's standards were not very exacting. He told me that he and his men did not discriminate, but would go after any ship hapless enough to wander into their sights. And despite their ostensible purpose of protecting Somali national waters, during the heat of the chase they paid no regard to international boundaries, pursuing their target until they caught it or it escaped them. Boyah separated his seafaring prey into the broad dichotomy of commercial and tourist ships. The commercial ships, identifiable by the cranes visible on their decks, were much slower and easier to capture. Boyah had gone after too many of these to remember: "a lot" was his most precise estimate.

He claimed to employ different tactics for different ships, but the basic strategy was crude in its simplicity. In attack groups spread amongst several small and speedy skiffs, Boyah and his men approached their target on all sides, swarming like a water-borne wolf pack. They brandished their weapons in an attempt to frighten the ship's crew into stopping, and even fired into the air. If these scare tactics did not work, and if the target ship was capable of outperforming their outboard motors, the chase ended there. But if they managed to pull even with their target, they tossed hooked rope ladders onto the decks and boarded the ship. Instances of the crew fighting back were rare, and rarely effective, and the whole process, from spotting to capturing, took at most thirty minutes. Boyah guessed that only 20 per cent to 30 per cent of attempted hijackings

met with success, for which he blamed speedy prey, technical problems, and foreign naval or domestic intervention.

The captured ship was then steered to a friendly port—in
Boyah's case, Eyl—where guards and interpreters were brought from
the shore to look after the hostages during the ransom negotiation.
Once the ransom was secured—often routed through banks in London and Dubai and parachuted like a special-delivery care package
directly onto the deck of the ship—it was split amongst all the concerned parties. Half the money went to the attackers, the men who
actually captured the ship. A third went to the operation's investors:
those who fronted the money for the ships, fuel, tracking equipment,
and weapons. The remaining sixth went to everyone else: the guards
ferried from shore to watch over the hostage crew, the suppliers of
food and water, the translators (occasionally high school students
on their summer break), and even the poor and disabled in the local
community, who received some as charity. Such largesse, Boyah told
me, had made his merry band into Robin Hood figures amongst the
residents of Eyl.

I asked Boyah where his men obtained the training to operate
their ships and equipment.

"Their training," he facetiously quipped, "has come from famine."
But this epigram, however pithy, did not contain the whole truth.
Beginning in 1999, the government of Puntland had launched a
series of ill-fated attempts to establish an (official) regional coast
guard, efforts that each ended with the dissolution of the contracting
company and the dismissal of its employees. The origin of the new
generation of Somali pirates—better trained, more efficiently organized, and possessing superior equipment—can be traced in part to
these failed coast-guarding experiments; with few other opportunities for their skills, many ex-coast-guard recruits turned to piracy.
When pressed, Boyah confirmed that some of his own men had past
histories in the Puntland Coast Guard, having joined his group after
their salaries went unpaid.

Boyah's testimony revealed another detail of the interwoven

dynamic between pirates, coast guards, and fishermen. Far from being a neutral state actor, the Puntland Coast Guard of the late 1990s and early 2000s worked as a private militia for the protection of commercial trawlers in possession of "fishing licences"—informal documents arbitrarily sold by various government bureaucrats for personal profit. The Puntland Coast Guard thus further alienated local fishermen, and indeed escalated at times into open confrontation with them. Boyah recounted that in 2001 his men seized several fishing vessels "licensed" by then-president Abdullahi Yusuf and protected by his coast guard force. Almost a decade before the fierce acceleration in pirate hijackings hit the Gulf of Aden, the conditions for the coming storm were already recognizable.

* * *

Boyah's moral compass seemed to be divided between sea and shore; he warned me, half-jokingly, not to run into him in a boat, but, despite my earlier misgivings, assured me that he was quite harmless on land. "We're not murderers," he said. "We've never killed anyone, we just attack ships."

He insisted that he knew what he was doing was wrong, and, as evidence of his sincerity, relayed how he had just appeared on the local news radio station, Radio Garowe, to call a temporary cease-fire on all pirate activity. Though I was sceptical that he wielded the authority necessary to enforce his decree amongst the wide range of decentralized groups operating over a coastline stretching almost sixteen hundred kilometres, Boyah stressed that the decision had been made by the Central Committee—and woe to those who defied its orders. "We will deal with them," Boyah promised. "We will work with the government forces to capture them and bring them to jail."

Subsequent events quickly proved that Boyah's radio statement was just so much background radiation. Just days after his announced ceasefire, a pirate gang in the Gulf of Aden committed the first commercial hijacking of 2009, capturing a German liquid petroleum tanker along with her thirteen crew members. The Central Committee has wreaked no vengeance on those responsible.

Boyah himself had not gone on a mission for over two months, for which he had a two-pronged explanation: "I got sick, and became rich." His fortune made, Boyah's call to end hijackings came from a position of luxury that most others did not enjoy. I questioned Boyah on whether his ceasefire had been at least partially motivated by the NATO task force recently deployed to deal with him and his colleagues.

"No," he said, "it has nothing to do with that. It's a moral issue. We started to realize that we were doing the wrong thing, and that we didn't have public support." Their public support, according to Boyah, had taken a plunge last summer when a delegation of local clan and religious leaders visited Eyl and declared to the local population that dealing with pirates was *haram*—religiously forbidden.

The current NATO deliberations regarding possible missile strikes on Eyl did not seem to concern Boyah. "Only civilians live there, it would be illegal for them to attack," he paused, before continuing, "if they do . . . that's okay. We believe in God." Forgetting for the moment his erstwhile promise of a ceasefire, Boyah's tone suddenly turned vehemently passionate. "Force alone cannot stop us," he said, "we don't care about death." Boyah's vocal display of courage was not idle bravado, but the plausible truth of a starkly desperate man. His desperation was not as stark as before he had accumulated his small fortune, but how long his current state of affluence would last was unclear—Boyah announced with pride that he had given his money away to his friends and to the poor, and that he hadn't built a house or a hotel like many of his more frugal colleagues.

As for his plans for the future, Boyah refused to give a straight answer. "That is up to the international community," he said. "It needs to solve the problem of illegal fishing, the root of our troubles. We are waiting for action."

* * *

Throughout our conversation, Boyah had been gazing off into space between my questions, looking bored. Soon he grew restless, mumbling discontentedly as he glanced at the two o'clock sun that "the day is already over." I managed to slip in one final question, asking him for his most exhilarating high seas chase. He immediately brightened up and launched into the story of the *Golden Nori,* a Japanese chemical tanker he had captured in October 2007 about fourteen kilometres off the northern Somali coast.

"Almost immediately after we had boarded the ship the US Navy surrounded it," said Boyah, with the destroyer USS *Porter* the first to respond. Boyah's memory, perhaps augmented with time, recalled seven naval vessels encircling him. Clearly he had told this story before; with obvious pride, Boyah recited by rote the identification numbers marking the sides of four of the vessels: 41, 56, 76, and 78 (the last being the designation of the *Porter*). The swiftness and gravity of this response nearly spooked Boyah's men into fleeing the ship and attempting an escape in their overmatched fishing skiffs. Fortunately for them, the *Golden Nori* was carrying volatile chemicals, including the extremely flammable compound benzene. With mirth lighting up his face, Boyah told me how the American ships were too afraid to fire on the ship for fear of detonating its payload, seemingly undisturbed by the fact that had his assessment been incorrect, he and his men would have been incinerated.

The standoff dragged on through November and into December. "We ran out of food," Boyah said, "and we almost abandoned the ship so we wouldn't start eating the crew." Attack helicopters whirring overhead, Boyah ordered the ship into the harbour at Bossaso, Puntland's most populous city. In case the *Nori*'s explosive cargo proved an insufficient deterrent, Boyah added the defensive screen provided by the presence of the city's civilian population.

His perseverance paid off. After lengthy negotiations aboard an American vessel, a pirate delegation finally secured a generous ransom of $1.5 million in exchange for releasing the *Nori* and its captive crew. As part of the deal, the American military guaranteed Boyah and his team safe passage off the hijacked ship. Puntland security forces, waiting on shore to arrest the brigands, could only watch as US Navy helicopters escorted the pirate skiffs to land and allowed the pirates to disembark. I asked Boyah why the Americans had let them escape once they had left the safety of their hostages on board the *Nori*.

"Because that was the agreement," Boyah said. But I already knew the real reason, at least from the US point of view: the Americans would not have known what to do with Boyah and his men if they had captured them. According to international law—to the extent that international law has any meaning in an utterly failed state—the Americans were not even supposed to be in Somali territorial waters. Their hands were tied, and they let the pirates go. (A diplomatic cable later released by the controversial, whistle-blowing WikiLeaks.org revealed that the US Navy's interest in the *Nori* had stemmed from fears that the ship had been hijacked by terrorists who intended to use the ship and its explosive cargo as a waterborne suicide bomb.)

The *Golden Nori* was one of the first major commercial vessels hijacked in the Gulf of Aden, before the international community had truly become cognizant of the problem. During this period, foreign navies tended to give pirates a slap on the wrist: their weapons and boats were impounded or destroyed, and they were released. More recently, states have begun to use the international legal instruments available to them—particularly a UN Security Council resolution permitting foreign entry into Somali waters—much more rigorously. Foreign warships are increasingly interdicting, detaining, and rendering suspected pirates to neighbouring countries to face justice.

Boyah had experienced this approach as well. In April 2008, his gang seized a rare prize, a speedy French luxury yacht on route from the Seychelles to the Mediterranean. Boyah called it the "*Libant*," a clumsy fusion of the ship's French name, *Le Ponant*. After delivering a ransom and freeing the hostages, French attack helicopters tracked the pirates inland to the village of Jariban. On the executive orders of President Nicolas Sarkozy, French commandos launched Operation Thalathine: special forces snipers disabled the pirates' getaway vehicle and captured six of the brigands, subsequently flying them to Paris to face trial. Such a determined, and exceedingly costly, pursuit was a rarity. But the incident illustrated that the international community was starting to take piracy in the Gulf of Aden more seriously—as well as showcasing the touchiness of French pride.

But a military solution alone is incapable of completely eradicating piracy off the Somali coast—nor is one either economically or politically feasible. Boyah's men had been captured or killed with increasing frequency in recent days (his brother was sitting in a Bossaso prison), but it did not matter. Imprisoning them was like trying to use a bailer to drain the ocean: for each pirate captured by the authorities, there were dozens of desperate young men on shore ready to rush in and fill the void.

* * *

Boyah had become visibly irritable, and the next pause in my questioning heralded the end of the interview. His bothersome task completed, he rose and started heading back to where the vehicles were parked. As he walked, Warsame casually sidled up to Boyah and slipped him a folded hundred-dollar bill; suddenly the puzzling incongruity between Boyah's irascible manner and his willingness to speak to me was perfectly clear. "These pirates always need money, you know, to buy khat," said Warsame, referring to the stimulant drug religiously consumed by pirates. "Always, they chew khat."

Meanwhile, Boyah had once more leaked out ahead of the rest of us, bounding up the trail alone. Warsame and I gaped as he suddenly took off and effortlessly cleared the metre-wide knee-high bramble patch separating the farm from the shoulder of the highway. With gigantic strides, he ran up the slope to the cars and waited impatiently as we slowly climbed up after him.

It was time for his khat.

2

A Short History of Piracy

SOMALIA WAS NOT ALWAYS THIS WAY. THE COUNTRY OF FAMINE and bloodshed, the lawless land where Boyah and his accomplices, like the pirates of yore, have been able to operate virtually unmolested, is the result of one of the most dramatic state collapses in modern history.

On October 15, 1969, the Somali Republic's second democratically elected president, Abdirashid Ali Shermarke, was shot and killed in the northern town of Las Anod by his own bodyguard. Though he was never proved to have ordered the assassination, army chief General Mohamed Siad Barre quickly initiated a bloodless coup that brought him to power for the next two decades.

Siad Barre was not a country person. Holding a profound contempt for the nation's nomadic traditions, he forcibly relocated whole populations of herders into collective settlements and communal farms. In his relentless drive to urbanize the country, Siad Barre directed virtually all government investment towards the capital, Mogadishu, which contained Somalia's only hospitals, universities, and professional opportunities. The city became a magnet for Somalia's diverse clans, drawing a cross-section of inhabitants from their traditional tribal homelands. For all his misdeeds, Siad Barre turned Mogadishu into the jewel of the Horn of Africa, a modern cosmopolis that attracted tourists from all over the world. The northern desert, conversely, was treated by the regime as a sterile and unproductive backwater.

In the late 1980s, Somalia erupted into civil war. Years of disastrous military campaigns, backward Marxist economic policies, and clan-based discrimination caused an increasingly isolated Siad Barre to fall back on a combination of his Marehan clan network and brutal repression by his security forces. Rebel groups, formed more or less along clan lines, descended on Mogadishu from all sides: the Somali National Movement drawn from the Isaaq clans of Somaliland, the Darod-dominated Somali Salvation Democratic Front (SSDF) operating from present-day Puntland, and the Hawiye United Somali Congress (USC) based in the south.

Siad Barre did not mince words with his adversaries: "When I came to Mogadishu . . . there was one road built by the Italians. If you try to force me to stand down, I will leave Mogadishu as I found it," he threatened. Sadly, he did even worse; when he finally fled Mogadishu in 1991, Siad Barre left the city in chaos.

Following Siad Barre's defeat, Mogadishu was left in the hands of USC warlord Mohamed Farah Aidid, a man best known as the target of the manhunt that culminated in the infamous "Black Hawk Down" incident, in which eighteen US Army Rangers lost their lives. Taking retribution for Siad Barre's persecution of their own clan, Aidid's Hawiye militias hunted down and massacred Darod civilians in the streets. In his book *The Zanzibar Chest*, former Reuters correspondent Aidan Hartley describes in chilling detail the life-and-death importance of clan lineage during the worst days of the war:

> A queue of civilians was huddled at a roadblock before a gang of rebels. As each person was waved through, another came forward and began uttering a litany of names. My guide with the flaming red hair said the people were reciting their clan family trees. The genealogies tumbled back generation after generation to a founding ancestor. It was like a DNA helix, or a fingerprint, or an encyclopedia of peace treaties and blood debts left to fester down the torrid centuries. I was thinking how poetic this idea was,

when bang!, a gunman shot one of the civilians, who fell with blood gush-
ing from his head and was pushed aside onto a heap of corpses.

"Wrong clan," said my flaming-haired friend. "He should have bor-
rowed the ancestors of a friend." [1]

If not quite as inborn as DNA or fingerprints, amongst Somalis the concept of clan operates almost like a mental grammar, an
innate neural structure that defines how one processes and inter-
prets the world. Before Siad Barre's time, it had been customary for
a Somali to greet someone he was meeting for the first time with the
question *Yaa tahay?* "What clan are you?" In his efforts to weaken
the clan system (and thereby buttress loyalty to the state), Siad Barre
outlawed the question, but to little effect; to this day, clan strongly
determines how Somalis assess one another's social position, moti-
vations, and trustworthiness.

Like the Bedouin, Somalis have traditionally been pastoral-
ists, their resource-poor desert environment giving rise to a rigid
and strictly territorial tribal system in which members are fiercely
defended and outsiders ruthlessly attacked. Indeed, the oft-quoted
Bedouin saying "Me against my brother; my brother and I against
my cousin; my brother, my cousin, and I against the world" could
well be adapted to Somalis: "My sub-sub-clan against my sub-clan,
my sub-clan against my clan, my clan against the world." In order to
avoid mutually destructive vendettas, a system of clan law, known as
heer, developed to resolve disputes through traditional rules of blood
compensation, which stipulate the number of camels, goats, and so
on paid to expiate each offence. The murder of a man, for instance,
would demand a restitution of one hundred camels (the equivalent
of about $20,000); a woman, fifty camels.

Despite Siad Barre's attempts to dismantle traditional patterns
of Somali life, clan loyalty remained a more dominant force than
Somali national identity, to the point where it eventually tore the
country apart. In a sense, the whole idea of Somalia was a contra-
diction—an attempt to graft the trappings of a modern state onto a

mode of social organization suited to a centuries-old nomadic life-style. Jobs, business opportunities, military appointments, government posts, and patronage were all awarded through clan networks, reinforcing ethnic divisions and undermining the legitimacy of the central state. Ironically—given its role in sparking Somalia's descent into civil war—the clan system has since ensured a degree of order and social cohesion in many areas, including Puntland and Somaliland, that otherwise might easily have degenerated into their own versions of Rwanda or the Democratic Republic of the Congo. For a country in "anarchy," law and order in some parts of Somalia is remarkably well-preserved.

* * *

Many of the Darod lucky enough to escape Mogadishu's urban killing fields fled north to their ancestral clan homeland, which at the time was under the control of the SSDF, headed by the squabbling duo of Colonel Abdullahi Yusuf Ahmed and General Mohamed Abshir. Towns that had been little more than underpopulated crossroads along nomadic migration routes swelled into urban centres. In the years following the outbreak of the civil war, Garowe grew from a population of five thousand to a current estimated thirty to forty thousand.[2]

Though the desert provided a safe haven against the persecution suffered by the Darod in the south, without political unity they remained vulnerable. Leaders of the Harti Confederacy (see Appendix 1), a grouping of the three Darod sub-clans inhabiting Puntland (the Majerteen, Dhulbahante, and Warsangali), looked on with apprehension at the formation of clan polities around them. With the Isaaq-inhabited self-declared Republic of Somaliland to their western flank and the Hawiye poised to extend their control from Mogadishu to much of south-central Somalia, the fear was that without a unified front the Darod would be at a disadvantage in the clan-centred scramble for Somalia's territories.

In May 1998, a conference of Harti clan elders in Garowe proclaimed the creation of Puntland State of Somalia, with Abdullahi Yusuf as its first president.[3] Unlike Somaliland, Puntland did not seek outright independence, but officially maintained its intention to join a future federal Somali state (albeit on its own terms). However, the international community has yet to officially recognize Puntland's status as a semi-autonomous region, and its relations with both the internationally recognized Transitional Federal Government (TFG) and Somaliland have been tense, and at times openly hostile.

For six years following the Garowe conference, Yusuf ruled Puntland as his personal fiefdom. When a 2001 election produced a victory for Yusuf's challenger, Jama Ali Jama, Yusuf did not bother to contest the results; he declared war, defeating Jama over the course of a six-month conflict. It was a rare outbreak of violence in a region that, since its founding, had remained largely insulated from the ongoing instability in southern Somalia.

In 2004, Yusuf headed south to take over the reins of the recently formed Somali TFG, handing over Puntland (after a three-month interim) to former general Mohamud Muse Hersi—a man known by the nickname of Adde Muse, or "White Moses." Hersi remained in power until January 2009, when Abdirahman Farole, an academic who had spent most of the previous twenty years in Melbourne, captured 74 per cent of the vote in an indirect presidential election held by Puntland's "parliament"—a collection of clan elders appointed from the region's seven districts. During and following the election, Farole took a hard-line stance against the buccaneers plying the region's waters, whom he viewed as a black mark on Puntland's international reputation: "The pirates are spoiling our society," he announced to the press following his victory. "We will crush them."[4]

It was a promise he has found difficult to fulfil.

* * *

By the time Farole assumed office in early 2009, sea banditry had become Puntland's only claim to recognition on the international stage. Yet piracy had existed as a Somalia-wide phenomenon since the outbreak of the civil war. As the central government collapsed on land, its ability to control its seas declined commensurately, and a varied assortment of militiamen, fishermen, and dregs of the Somali army all seized advantage. Like darts striking a map, pirate attacks occurred up and down the length of the Somali coast, indifferent to geographical location. These early operations were sporadic, opportunistic, and unsophisticated—little more than groups of gunmen floating in four-metre skiffs a few kilometres away from the shore, waiting for wayward vessels to stray too close. The use of far-ranging "motherships" (fishing dhows or other larger vessels employed as floating bases of operations) was not yet common, and these nascent pirates did not typically venture far beyond the hundred or so miles constituting the traditional sphere of Somali fishermen—well short of international shipping lanes. By consequence, their victims were typically fishing trawlers, whose search for lobster and demersal (bottom-dwelling) fish required them to come close to shore.

The attacks most frequently took the form of "marine muggings," during which the brigands would board the vessel and steal money and everything else of easily transportable value before quickly departing. Like muggings, they sometimes turned violent, as was the case in the very first recorded act of modern piracy in Somalia—an incident that marked the closest the Somali pirates have come to the seventeenth-century stereotype of bloodthirsty buccaneers.

On January 12, 1991, the cargo ship *Naviluck* was boarded by three boatloads of armed pirates off the Puntland coast near the town of Hafun while en route from Mombasa to Jeddah. The pirates took three of the vessel's Filipino crewmen ashore and summarily executed them, before forcing the remaining crew to jump overboard and setting the *Naviluck* ablaze. Only by the grace of a passing trawler were the floundering victims of this "plank walking" saved from the fate of their three comrades.

Not all hijackings were carried out by these sorts of water-borne thugs; some had a veneer of legality. The hodgepodge of rebel groups, militias, and warlords that had inherited chunks of the Somali state (along with the remnants of its navy) began to arrest foreign fishing vessels and extort "fines" for their release. In Puntland, one of the men given this assignment was Abdiwahid Mahamed Hersi, known as Joaar, the owner of a small-scale lobster fishing company who had once employed, as one of his divers, none other than the young Boyah. In 1993, as the civil war continued to rage in the south, Abdullahi Yusuf instructed Joaar to end illegal fishing by foreign fleets off SSDF-controlled territory. In response to this command, Joaar told me, he hired a boat at $200 per day and recruited thirty young men to serve as his marines (I was unable to discover if Boyah was amongst them). According to Joaar's reckoning, he and his men stopped a total of nine Pakistani dhows, bringing them to Bossaso and ransoming three of them back to their home government (there are even rumours, which Joaar denies, that he and his colleagues hijacked a ship out of Mombasa harbour by smuggling a pistol on board in the bottom of a fruit basket). His actions had the desired effect, or so he believed. "Our seas became very clean at that time," Joaar said.

Though he had originally planned to create a full-fledged coast guard, Joaar found himself unable to complete the task. Illegal fishing ships, he said, were under the protection of southern warlords, who took exception to the harassment of their clients. "People were calling my home phone and threatening me," he explained, a fact that helped convince him to shelve his long-term plans.

Acting as he was under orders from the SSDF—the authority in de facto control of the territory at the time—Joaar's exploits are perhaps better described as semi-legitimate privateering rather than outright piracy. In either case, the man some call "the father of piracy" has since put his hijacking past behind him, though he has remained true to his maritime calling: Joaar is currently the director general of the Puntland Ministry of Fisheries, a position he has held since 2004.

* * *

In 1995, two years after the commissioning of Joaar's improvised coast guard, Boyah, Garaad Mohammed (another of Eyl's early pirate leaders), and other Eyl fishermen unleashed their own vigilante brigade upon the seas. At least, 1995 is the starting date Boyah gave me; Stig Jarle Hansen, a Norwegian Puntland specialist who has conducted his own interviews with Boyah, reported him as claiming that "professional piracy" had begun in 1994, but that his group had been engaged in struggles with foreign trawlers as early as 1992. (Momman, one of Boyah's former lieutenants, later told me that the group had begun operations back in 1991.)[5]. The public record lends some credence to Hansen's version of events, showing a sharp rise in both pirate attacks and hijackings in 1994, though the total number of hijackings (four) remained very low.[6]

Boyah and his colleagues were the original models for the oft-invoked media image of the fisherman-pirate locked in a one-sided struggle against the forces of foreign exploitation. They certainly cultivated this impression; if Boyah is to be believed, his operations were directed solely against foreign fishing trawlers, though this claim could easily have been influenced by the desire to justify his actions to the outside world. His tactics were still relatively basic; Boyah repeatedly denied to me that he or his men had ever used motherships, saying they stayed relatively close to shore in their fishing skiffs. Hansen's research attests to this limited range; from 1991 to 1995, almost half of all pirate attacks occurred in Puntland waters, while fewer than one-sixth took place on the high seas.[7]

In 2003, Somali piracy underwent a metamorphosis, thanks to the vision of a complete outsider: Mohamed Abdi Hassan, known as Afweyne ("Big Mouth"), a former civil servant from the distant central coastal town of Harardheere. Drawing on his fellow Habir Gedir clan members (a branch of the Hawiye), Afweyne formed the Somali Marines, an organization that transformed his hometown and its southern neighbour Hobyo—which had hitherto spawned relatively little pirate activity—into the centre of the pirate world.

A capitalist at heart, Afweyne was the first to realize the potential of piracy as a business, and went about raising venture funds for his pirate operations as if he were launching a Wall Street IPO. One repentant potential investor recalled Afweyne's sales pitch: "He asked me to invest USD 2,000, as he was gathering money for his new business venture. He was begging . . . [but] I did not invest and I regret it so much today." [8]

Like any conscientious employer, Afweyne sought to provide the very best training for his employees. Though the old boys of Eyl belonged to the rival Majerteen clan, Afweyne was not one to allow tribalism to get in the way of business, and he personally recruited the most locally renowned pirates—including Boyah and Garaad Mohammed—to work as instructors. The Eyl veterans did not limit their role to that of mere consultants but travelled up and down the coast, organizing and even participating in pirate operations. Even in 2007–2008, after most of the Eyl pirate leaders had returned to Puntland—attracted by the easy hunting offered in the Gulf of Aden—piracy remained the incestuous province of the Majerteen and Habir Gedir clans. Boyah, during our numerous conversations, was not shy about discussing the Eyl–Harardheere connection, readily speaking about "joint operations" between the two groups; one such collaborative effort was the hijacking of the MV *Faina*, the tank-laden Ukrainian transport ship that first splashed Somali piracy across international headlines. Boyah was upfront about Afweyne's business acumen: "Afweyne hand picked his pirate group," he later testified, "carefully designed it to keep costs low, profits high and to maximize efficiency." [9]

In contrast to previous groups, the Somali Marines were extremely well organized, employing a military-style hierarchy with titles such as fleet admiral, admiral, vice admiral, and head of financial operations (Afweyne himself). [10] They exhibited an operational sophistication that matched their corporate professionalism, employing motherships that extended their attack radius hundreds of kilometres from the coast.

Around the same time, other professionally organized groups began to appear. Garaad Mohammed was not content to remain as Afweyne's underling, but formed his own organization, the National Volunteer Coast Guard (NVCG), in the major southern port of Kismaayo.[11] Not only were groups like the NVCG and the Somali Marines more sophisticated in an operational sense, their creative names—which cast them as the defenders of Somali waters against the imperialist incursions of foreign vessels—showed that their PR acumen was keeping pace.

But though their official raison d'être might have been to prevent the theft of Somalia's fish, the Somali Marines showed no shame in attacking those whose intentions were quite the opposite. From 2005 to 2007, the gang targeted World Food Programme (WFP) transports delivering vital food aid to the famine-stricken population of southern Somalia, attacking five vessels and hijacking at least two. Perhaps Afweyne was aware of his potential vulnerability to accusations of hypocrisy; following the seizure of the MV *Semlow* in June 2005, he claimed the vessel's 850-tonne cargo of rice in the name of the people of Harardheere, accusing the international community of neglecting the region.[12] The threat to WFP vessels did not disappear until late 2007, when the French navy began to escort the shipments to port.

As for Afweyne, he has since entered a comfortable semi-retirement, handing over many of the day-to-day operations of the family business to his son Abdulkhadar. Afweyne is perhaps one of the few men to fit the media stereotype of a cash-flush pirate kingpin, having allegedly converted his pirate earnings into a business empire stretching from India to Kenya. He has even enjoyed the dubious distinction of a state reception from eccentric former Libyan dictator Muammar Gaddafi, who had revealed a quixotic affection for the Somali pirates during his seventy-five-minute rant at the 2009 UN General Assembly world leaders' summit.

* * *

As a boil festers before it bursts, the 2003–2006 Eyl–Harardheere alliance represented an incubation period for the Somali pirates, a time during which they gradually accumulated capital and experience, continually reinvesting their ransom money in ongoing operations. By the 2008 explosion of piracy in the Gulf of Aden, the pirate business model had already been tried and tested, and sufficient cash was available from previous ransoms to provide gainful employment for the countless volunteers lining up on the beaches of Eyl.

For the poorly educated, locally born youth, the security sector, both public and private, had been the steadiest source of formal sector jobs. It came as a shock, then, when in April 2008 the Puntland government ran out of money to pay its security forces. Many members of the police and army naturally sought alternative employment, and there was hardly a more lucrative career than piracy for a young man possessing nothing but a gun and a desperate disregard for his own life.

Scant other opportunities were available. Puntland's almost non-existent factories provide only a handful of manufacturing jobs, and the already negligible seafood export industry had been suffering on account of both illegal foreign fishing and the decline of lobster stocks. Day labour in Puntland's rapidly expanding cities was one of the only avenues of steady employment open to the estimated 70 per cent of Puntlanders under the age of thirty. While much of the population (65 per cent, according to the Puntland government), remains nomadic, living a traditional pastoral lifestyle outside the formal economy, the increasing numbers of nomads flocking to urban centres in recent years have not found much to occupy their time other than the drug khat.

There *is* legitimate money to be made in Somalia. But the most lucrative business opportunities—livestock export, the transport and telecommunications industries, as well as jobs in government and the civil service—are monopolized by educated Somali expats, who speak English and Arabic and often split their time between Somalia and their adoptive homelands. The result has been a gross socioeconomic gap between those who were able to escape the civil war and those who were forced to remain in Somalia and suffer the brunt of the violence. For the masses of unemployed and resentful local youth, piracy was a quick way to achieve the respect and standard of living that the circumstances of their birth had denied them.

* * *

Before the presence of the massive naval flotillas that now jam Somali coastal waters, the risks were fewer, but the payouts were also relatively paltry. One of the Somali Marines' most noteworthy prizes in the early days was the MV *Feisty Gas*, a Hong Kong–flagged liquid petroleum tanker captured in April 2005. In exchange for her release, the Marines received a mere $315,000, likely about one-tenth the sum they might have received five years down the line. Since then, ransom amounts have crept steadily higher, with each new precedent exerting an upward pressure on future payments. At the time of writing, the highest recorded ransom had reached a staggering $13.5 million, paid in February 2011 to free the oil super-tanker *Irene SL*.

Later generations of pirates owed their extravagant multimillion-dollar ransoms to the negotiating abilities of the pioneers. Indeed, the triumvirate of Afweyne, Boyah, and Garaad Mohammed could be compared to the hard-nosed leaders of a newly formed labour union—though in their struggle for higher wages they admittedly employed stronger-arm tactics than typically seen in collective bargaining. The lucrative ransoms for which they fought predictably attracted a new influx of independent groups to the industry—what I refer to as the "third wave" of piracy in Puntland. Many of these pirates were opportunists without histories in fishing, often disaffected inland youth. Yet their recent entry into the field did not stop them from telling any apologist reporter who would listen that per-

secution by foreign fishing fleets had driven them to their desperate
course.

* * *

Harardheere's piracy dominance temporarily came to an end in
2006, when the Islamic Courts Union—an Islamist political movement—seized control of the south of the country and cracked down
on pirate operations, claiming that the practice violated Islamic law.
This paved the way for piracy to relocate to the next logical locale:
back to Puntland, the gateway to the Gulf of Aden. From 2007 to
2008, Eyl was the undisputed capital of the Somali pirate empire,
until the establishment of the heavily patrolled maritime safety corridor in the Gulf of Aden allowed Harardheere to reclaim the title in
late 2009.

International recognition of the problem was sluggish. Though
mariners in Somali waters had for years been keeping their eyes
nervously glued to their radar displays, the triple intrigue of arms,
oil, and Americans was needed for the Somali pirates to make international news headlines. The galvanizing event was the September
2008 seizure of the Ukrainian transport ship *Faina,* which combined
the mystique of high-seas buccaneers and international weapons
trafficking: in contravention of a UN embargo, the *Faina* was carrying Soviet-era tanks destined for southern Sudan, likely with the full
knowledge of the Kenyan government. Two months later came the
daring hijacking of the MV *Sirius Star,* a Saudi supertanker carrying
$100 million in crude oil; seized a shocking eight hundred and fifty
kilometres southeast of Somalia, the incident marked the furthest
the Somali pirates had ventured out to sea at the time. Finally, in
April 2009, pirates attacked the *Maersk Alabama,* the first American cargo vessel to be hijacked in two centuries. A tense three-day
standoff with an American warship, worthy of a Hollywood script,
ended with three Navy SEAL sniper bullets to the hijackers' heads
and the lone survivor brought back to face US justice in a New York
courtroom. The *Alabama* incident catapulted Somali sea piracy to

the attention of the American public, and convinced editors around the world that the pirates were worthy of their front pages.

This trinity of hijackings that seized the imagination of the average news consumer were the brainchildren of the founding fathers of Somali piracy: the *Faina* was a joint operation between Boyah's and Garaad Mohammed's gangs and the Somali Marines, the *Sirius Star* hijacking was carried out by Afweyne's group alone, and the *Alabama* attack was publicly claimed by Garaad.[13]

The Somali pirates had come of age.

* * *

The basic characteristics that made Puntland an ideal spawning ground for pirates had existed since its founding in 1998. Why, then, did it take ten years for piracy to develop into the present epidemic? Four main causes explain the rise of piracy in Puntland: geopolitics, environmental factors, economic adversity, and breakdown of governance (two other principal factors, illegal fishing and toxic dumping, and the Puntland Coast Guard, will be discussed in Chapter 4).

In geopolitical terms, two factors lent Puntland a comparative advantage in the piracy "industry": its location and its relative (but tenuous) stability. The benefit of its geography is readily apparent: situated right at the intersection of the Indian Ocean and the Gulf of Aden, Puntland straddles one of the busiest shipping lanes in the world. More than 20,000 commercial vessels, or about 10 per cent of global shipping, transit through the Gulf of Aden each year.

Second, Puntland's isolation from the ongoing civil war in the south as well as its semi-functioning government ensured that pirate organizers would be left in relative peace to plan and carry out their operations. Piracy is not so much organized crime as it is a business, characterized by extremely efficient capital flows, low start-up costs, and few entry barriers. Pirates, almost as much as businessmen, require a certain level of order and predictability for their enterprises to prosper (and to avoid getting ripped off by actual organized crime networks). Roger Middleton, a Horn of Africa expert with the London-based think tank Chatham House, summed it up eloquently for me: "Puntland was the perfect area for pirates to operate because it's just stable enough, but also ungoverned enough. You don't have the chronic instability you have further south . . . There's too great a chance of getting caught in the crossfire and too many competing interests to pay off."

The link between political stability and the frequency of pirate attacks has some convincing empirical support; when Puntland descended into violence, piracy was the first business to suffer. In 1992, for instance, the year when Abdullahi Yusuf was locked in a fierce conflict to prevent the Islamist organization al-Ittihad al-Islami from establishing a Puntland foothold, piracy completely disappeared from the region. In 1994–1995, after Yusuf had triumphed and relative peace was restored, the frequency of pirate attacks began to creep up once more.[14]

The theory holds for Harardheere and Hobyo as well, which are located in another autonomous region—Galmudug—insulated from the chaotic south. Galmudug, with an administration far weaker than even Puntland's, was perhaps an even more ideal business environment for pirate entrepreneurs—a fact that the astute Afweyne was able to capitalize on.

Somaliland, in contrast, possesses a Gulf of Aden coastline comparable to Puntland's, yet the few pirates originating from the region have been swiftly arrested and incarcerated by the local authorities. The difference is due to Somaliland's greater political stability, a product of its robust history of democracy and inter-clan consensus. Its central government can exert control over its territory in a way that Puntland's leaders, who must navigate a much more fractured clan landscape, cannot. In the south, in short, the pirates had to fear other criminals; in Somaliland, the danger came from a more traditional source: the police.

Environmental circumstances also contributed to the rise of piracy. The population of Puntland is largely nomadic, and depends heavily on the seasonal rains to sustain their livestock herds. From 2002 to 2004, Puntland suffered its worst drought in thirty years. Herds were decimated, and much of the nomadic population flocked to urban centres in search of food. With an estimated 600,000 across Somalia directly affected by the dry spell, the governments of both Puntland and Somaliland declared a humanitarian emergency. Although there is no conclusive evidence, it is possible that this drought drove those traditionally dependent on livestock to rely on fishing as a source of sustenance, with the result that the standard encroachment by foreign fleets on Somali fisheries may have been viewed as especially egregious.

Just as Puntland was on the verge of recovery from this crippling drought, Mother Nature supplied her own solution to the water shortage. On December 26, 2004, one of the most powerful tsunamis in recorded history struck near the Indonesian island of Sumatra, sending waves as high as thirty metres surging across the Indian Ocean. The coastal areas of Puntland—though more than 4,800 kilometres from the tsunami's epicentre—did not escape. Over three hundred people were killed and the livelihoods of forty-four thousand affected.[15] The tsunami devastated the region's fishing economy, destroying an estimated six hundred boats and damaging 75 per cent of the fishing gear beyond repair.[16]

One of the tsunami's indirect contributions to the piracy outbreak was the (literal) exposure of toxic dumping in Somali waters. Residents of Eyl and nearby coastal towns related how the tsunami's waves had broken open and scattered ashore previously submerged toxic waste canisters, causing an increase in the incidence of radiation sicknesses amongst the local population. Though a brief UN fact-finding mission to the area found no evidence to corroborate these claims, the perception that foreign nations have used Somalia as a toxic dumping ground has served as both a rallying cry and a post hoc justification for the pirate movement.

The four-year delay between the drought and tsunami and the outbreak of piracy makes it difficult to finger them as immediate causes. But these environmental factors undoubtedly exacerbated the general level of poverty and suffering in Puntland, increasing the pool of candidates for pirate recruiters.[17]

Puntland's declining economy also provided an additional incentive to turn to piracy. From 2006 to 2008, the region experienced unbridled hyperinflation that drastically reduced the standard of living of the average citizen. Puntland still uses the shilling, the currency of the defunct Somali Republic, though only the highest denominations of five hundred and one thousand shillings remain in use (the latter bill is worth approximately three cents). While US dollars are used for larger transactions, shillings remain the staple choice for everyday purchases, and are typically exchanged in bundles of 100,000.

From a high of 14,000 shillings per US dollar in 2006, by August 2008 the exchange rate had fallen to a record low of 35,000 per dollar.[18] In Garowe, Bossaso, Qardho, and Galkayo, protesters filled the streets to express their anger over the rising price of goods, blocking roads and pelting government buildings with stones. General Hersi's administration responded with a desperate attempt to fix an exchange rate of 18,000 shillings per dollar, a measure that even a totalitarian state would have found difficult to enforce.

Counterfeiting was a problem I noticed almost immediately upon my arrival in Puntland. For a currency that had not been minted in almost two decades, it was astounding how many crisp thousand-shilling notes proclaimed "Mogadishu 1991" in unfaded orange ink. Indeed, nineteen out of twenty local bills looked as if they had been printed by a cheap photocopier. It was not until early 2009, when local sheikhs launched a campaign to dissuade the organizers of counterfeiting operations, that hyperinflation began to come under control; by March, the exchange rate had stabilized at 29,000 shillings per dollar.[19]

Puntland's economic woes were mirrored by the decline of its political institutions. As hyperinflation escalated, the salary of a regular soldier in the Darawish (the Puntland army) dropped almost threefold in real terms, from more than seventy dollars in 2006 to less than thirty dollars in 2008.[20] President Hersi continued to pay his forces in printed money until, in April 2008, he stopped paying them altogether. As mentioned above, many soldiers and policemen abandoned their positions and turned to piracy; a local crime wave ensued, and May saw the first increase in pirate attacks, a trend that took off following the end of the monsoon season in August.[21]

Prior to the discontinuation of its pay, the Darawish had already been depleted in raw numbers. When Puntland strongman Abdullahi Yusuf had accepted the post of president of Somalia's Transitional Federal Government (TFG) in 2004, he took about a thousand Puntland soldiers (out of an estimated five thousand) south to Mogadishu to serve as his personal militia, funded out of government revenue.[22] With this weakening of the security forces, the Puntland government's ability to project its power throughout its territory declined. "Puntland's capacity to investigate piracy onshore, always weak, had totally collapsed," writes Stig Hansen.[23]

Following Puntland's military decline, its always-tense relationship with its western neighbour, Somaliland, worsened precipitously; in October 2007, Somaliland forces invaded Puntland and captured the town of Las Anod, capital of the disputed Sool region. Though this invasion was not in itself a direct contributor to the piracy outbreak, it was indicative of the Puntland government's loss of control. Rival clans to the Osman Mahamoud-dominated administration, such as the Isse Mahamoud, began to assert their independence from the central government, and Isse Mahamoud–inhabited areas like Eyl became lawless enclaves ideal for pirate operations.

* * *

The history of Somali piracy has been, one might say, a tale of two cities: Eyl and Harardheere. Like the Paris and London Dickens wrote of, the towns were hotbeds of revolutionary sentiment, seething against oppression and injustice. In Eyl, a band of angry young twentysomethings headed by Boyah and Garaad Mohammed formed the simmering nucleus that developed into the modern Somali piracy movement. "Boyah was a pioneer," one local journalist told me. "He showed the others the real potential of piracy."

Puntland's semi-lawless status made the region an ideal training ground and business environment for the early pirates; relatively peaceful, it was free of the organized criminal gangs, Islamist groups, and covetous warlords that plagued the turbulent south. From 2005 to early 2009, as the central government disintegrated under increasing economic and political pressures, pirate groups gained the freedom to operate with complete openness and virtual impunity.

Yet much of the early history of Somali piracy is still clouded in obscurity. With few outside observers present on the ground, little reliable information about the country is available to academics and journalists, and many past (and present) pirate attacks go unreported by shipowners. This dearth of credible information has created an opening for conjecture and speculation, with the result that, as with the buccaneers of yesteryear, a number of present-day myths about the Somali pirates have already sprung up.

3

Pirate Lore

EDWARD TEACH (OR BLACKBEARD, AS HE IS MORE COMMONLY known) was reported to have tied sulphur fuses into his beard, which he would set alight before going into battle in order to give himself the appearance of the devil. It is said he liked to drink a burning mixture of gunpowder and rum, and that, after he was killed and decapitated by the Royal Navy, his skull was fashioned into a silver chalice. Another legend holds that the Barbary corsair Barbarossa ("Red Beard"), Blackbeard's North African predecessor, tortured the inhabitants of a small Greek island in order to discover the location of a town concealed by a precipitous gorge. As the bloodthirsty pirates descended upon the town, mothers threw their children over the edge of the cliff in order to save them from being sold into slavery.

Passed down through the centuries, such tales are probably as apocryphal as the stories of buried treasure, peg legs, and Jolly Roger flags, yet they have become part of our collective image of the swashbuckling buccaneer. Somalia's modern sea bandits may lack some of this colour, but, aided by the news media's inexorable search for a good yarn, they are already on their way to amassing their own canon of folklore.

MYTH #1: SOMALI WATERS ARE TEEMING WITH PIRATES.

In recent years, information technology has made twenty-four-hour-a-day news coverage a reality, with the unintended result of making the world seem much riskier than it is. Given the international media focus on every daring hijacking off the Somali coast, sailing through "Pirate Alley"—the shipping lane from the Indian Ocean through the Gulf of Aden—may appear as dangerous as a seventeenth-century trip across the Spanish Main in a gold-laden galleon. But before you abandon your plans for a career in the merchant marine, ask yourself, What are the actual chances of being hijacked by Somali pirates? When you switch off the six o'clock news and examine the numbers, they turn out not to be very high. In 2008, about twenty-four thousand commercial transits through the Gulf of Aden led to only forty-two successful hijackings, according to the International Maritime Bureau, a global body devoted to combating maritime crime.[1] In short, the average sailor faced *less than a 1 in 550 chance* (0.17 per cent) of being taken hostage on a given voyage—not all that much worse than the effectively 0 per cent chance on any other sea route in the world.

Of course, for some this figure will be significantly higher; to the poor sailor on a supertanker with a maximum speed of eight knots and a low freeboard, the Gulf of Aden might start to look uncomfortably similar to the Spanish Main.

MYTH #2: THE PIRATES ARE IN THE POCKETS OF SOMALI ISLAMISTS.

By all measures, Somalia should have been one of the most economically successful African nations: it has the continent's longest coastline, is strategically situated on the Suez Canal shipping lane, and has a long-standing history of trade and entrepreneurship. Sadly, events have taken the country along a different trajectory, and for the last two decades the international community has been trying a variety of strategies to piece it back together. Initially, the United Nations embraced the "building block" approach, which focused on supporting and engaging with the relatively stable mini-states within Somalia, such as Puntland and Somaliland. The logic was that if these regions became bastions of peace and security, their stability would spread to the more turbulent areas surrounding them. Once a number of such "blocks" were in place, reassembling a federal government would be a relatively easy task.

This all changed in 2000, when the Somali National Peace Conference held in Djibouti produced the Transitional National Government (TNG), an ultimately ineffectual attempt to restore central government to the country from the top down. After the TNG went bankrupt and collapsed, it was replaced in 2004 by the current Transitional Federal Government (TFG). Choosing to view these national reconciliation attempts as legitimate expressions of the will of the Somali people (despite the fact that Somaliland—representing a quarter of the nation's territory—continued to seek outright independence), the international community threw its backing behind the TFG.

International support for the central government became further entrenched in 2006, when Ethiopian troops disastrously invaded Somalia in order to overthrow the Islamic Courts Union (ICU), an Islamist political movement that had wrested control of Mogadishu and much of the south from the TFG and competing warlord factions. The Ethiopian intervention drove ICU's moderate leadership into exile and sparked a radicalization of the organization, as the ICU's extremist military wing, Al-Shabaab, splintered from the group and launched a brutal insurgency against the Ethiopian occupiers. The US government had already been wary of the ICU's Islamist ideology and its potential links to Al Qaeda, and had backed the Ethiopian invasion with air and logistical support; the emergence of Shabaab turned the TFG into a key ally in the war on terror. No longer was the TFG merely the latest phase of a strategically irrelevant country's struggle with anarchy, but the last bulwark against an Islamist takeover of the Horn of Africa. This perception was reinforced in March 2010, when Al-Shabaab officially declared its affiliation with Al Qaeda, and in July, when

Shabaab carried out its first suicide attack outside of Somalia, setting off bombs in two bars in Kampala, Uganda, packed with World Cup revellers.

Following the overthrow of the ICU, the TFG underwent another transformation. Under pressure from the international community, it merged with the Alliance for the Re-liberation of Somalia (ARS), an "opposition party" hastily formed by the self-proclaimed moderate ICU cadres who had fled into exile in Eritrea and Djibouti. The repentant Islamists were accommodated with 275 new seats in the Somali parliament, doubling it to an absurdly bloated 550 members. The leader of the ARS (and former ICU chief), Sheikh Sharif Ahmed, was elected president of the new body. Until Al-Shabaab withdrew from the capital city in August 2011, members of Sheikh Sharif's government had huddled in their Mogadishu barracks, their daily docket of business more concerned with surviving the continual onslaught of Shabaab militants than administering the country.

Drawn by YouTube videos, foreign jihadis have come flocking to Somalia from around the world, including Pakistan, Afghanistan, Canada, Britain, and the United States (Omar Hammami, known as Abu Mansoor "Al-Amriki," one of Shabaab's more notorious online recruiters, is a US citizen born in small-town Alabama). With its suppression of women, glorification of martyrdom, and visions of a global caliphate, Shabaab embraces the kind of Islam the war on terror thrives on. In the areas under its control, the group has banned sports, music, and even bras; those who transgress the group's strict Salafi interpretation of sharia law face amputation and medieval executions (girls as young as thirteen have been stoned to death for the "crime" of adultery).[2] Shabaab's radicalism was new to Somalis, who had traditionally practiced a moderate, Sufi-influenced variety of Islam. Up until a generation ago, it was common for women to uncover their heads; these days, the Arab style of dress, with its accompanying headscarf, is virtually ubiquitous.

In a world dominated by the discourse of the war on terror, various policy analysts, journalists, and politicians pushing particular agendas inevitably began to speculate about pirate cash ending up in the hands of terrorists. One of the early claims came from the London-based publication *Jane's Terrorism and Security Monitor,* which reported that Shabaab had provided the pirates with funds, bases, and "specialist weapons" in exchange for a share of the ransoms as well as pirate training in "naval tactics."[3] The image of turbaned Islamists instructing pirates in sharpshooting in return for sailing lessons would be laughable if it did not have such serious implications for the safety of hostages; a Shabaab-piracy connection would effectively prevent the paying of ransoms, since in most Western countries it is illegal under any circumstances to transfer funds to a designated terrorist organization.

History, at least, seems to be against those who would claim an Islamist-pirate conspiracy. In 2006, the Islamic Courts Union began pushing north, reaching Harardheere in August. Dubbing piracy un-Islamic, or *haram,* ICU militias shut down operations in Harardheere, forcing many pirates into Puntland (as mentioned in Chapter 2, the ICU clamp-down in Harardheere partly accounted for the rise of Eyl as Somalia's piracy capital). Despite the potential loss of revenue, evincing such an attitude—at least publicly—was necessary for the ICU to maintain the legitimacy of its fundamentalist ideology. It was able to afford its pious airs; the group reportedly receives substantial funding from affluent supporters in Saudi Arabia and the other Gulf states.

During my months in Puntland, I questioned every pirate I met about Islamist ties, and received the same vehement denials from every one. Nonetheless, some indications of a relationship between Al-Shabaab and the pirates had emerged by late 2009, or so said my source in the Somali diplomatic community. On October 2, the Spanish tuna boat *Alakrana* was seized by one of Afweyne's attack groups and brought to Harardheere (the thirty-six hostages were released seven weeks later for a reported ransom of $4.5 million). Before arriving in Harardheere, however, the pirates stopped at the Shabaab-controlled port of Baraawe, where two hijackers headed for shore in a small skiff. They had hardly left the ship before a Spanish navy helicopter intercepted and arrested them.

"They were supposed to meet the Shabaab leaders in Baraawe and bring them to Harardheere," my source explained. "As it turned out, the leaders had to make the trip by road." The incident, he argued, was "ultimate evidence" of a connection between Shabaab and the Harardheere pirates, a relationship that he said had been brokered by Afweyne himself. "Shabaab could be receiving anywhere from 5 per cent to 60 per cent of the ransom," my source said. "And according to my information, it's much more than a gentleman's agreement for money. Al-Shabaab itself seems to be training for acts of piracy—becoming, in effect, 'sea Mujahedeen.'"

Nevertheless, there is still no evidence, over two years later, that any Islamist group had launched a "piracy division." But this may change; in a repeat of the 2006 ICU clamp-down, Hizbul Islam—the then second most influential Islamist group in Somalia, after Shabaab—invaded Harardheere in May 2010, chasing many of the resident pirates north to the town of Hobyo. Like the ICU, both Hizbul Islam and Shabaab have publicly declared piracy to be *haram,* but the lure of large sums of money may have spawned a reinterpretation of the scriptures; there are reports that the remaining Harardheere pirates have begun to split their ransoms with both Islamist groups.[4] In the cynical words of my diplomat source, "Nothing is *haram* if it supports the insurgency."

In Hobyo, conversely, the pirates have decided to fight 'em rather than join 'em. Mohamed Garfanje, a Hobyo pirate strongman believed to have hijacked a half-dozen ships, has built up an organized militia consisting of several hundred men, eighty heavy machine guns, and six technicals (flatbed trucks mounted with light anti-aircraft guns).[5] In an effort to stave off the Islamist expansion, Garfanje has placed his muscle in the service of local officials of Galmudug, the semi-autonomous region in which Harardheere and Hobyo are located (the Galmudug administration, it must be said, has never exercised effective control over the towns).

Links between pirates and terrorists undoubtedly exist, but they are isolated and incidental—opportunistic individuals with Islamist ties who happen to dabble in piracy investments on the side. Shabaab, as an organization, does not yet have conclusive systematic links to the pirates, and the pirates have good reason to keep it that way. As one Somalia analyst put it to me: "If I'm a pirate and I'm giving money to Al-Shabaab, I can be pretty sure that some American is going to find out and drop a bomb on my head. It's simply a very, very bad business decision."

MYTH #3: SOMALI PIRACY IS RUN BY AN INTERNATIONAL CRIMINAL CARTEL.

Many theories have sprung up to explain the astounding success of the Somali pirates in snatching vessels from right under the guns of Western naval armadas, almost all of which seem to rest on the assumption that the Somalis could not possibly be doing it on their own. Security firms, media outlets, and law enforcement agencies have all alleged the existence of a vast and sophisticated international crime network providing funding, equipment, and intelligence to their local Somali minions—conjuring the image of a sinister Bond film villain pushing buttons on a giant maritime navigation display.

One of the strongest and most outlandish claims came in October 2009, when Interpol announced that Somali piracy was controlled by "transnational crime syndicates." "It is organized crime," Jean-Michel Louboutin, executive director of police services at Interpol, bluntly told the Agence France-Presse (when I attempted to contact Mr. Louboutin to clarify his statement, a public relations rep informed me, without elaborating, that he had been misquoted).[6]

I asked Toby Stephens, a London-based crisis response lawyer, about these claims. The principal function of Stephens's firm is to "convince" a hijacked ship's various insurers to put up the ransom money, and his job had taken him almost as far as the negotiating room during the ransom bargaining process. "We've been involved with various security services in tracing the pirates' phone calls, as well as their assets," said Stephens. "There have been definite instances of calls coming to telephones in London. The criminal network certainly extends beyond Somalia, but my perception is that it is not nearly as organized as people think," he continued. "I think the pirates are a disorganized bunch, but they do have contacts—friends, family, whoever it may be—in places around the globe. And they draw on those, but it's not a mafia-style organized crime network."

On the ground, there is little to back up the tales of international conspiracy. Pirates operate in relatively small, decentralized groups of twenty to fifty—essentially, relatives and friends who come together for the purpose of a mission, then disperse once the task is complete and the ransom has been divided up. The loyalty of the average pirate is to the money, not the Don.

Nor is there any evidence of the rivalries and turf wars one would expect in an organized crime environment. While isolated cases of gang infighting have resulted in deaths, no pirate organization maintains a standing "hit squad," and inter-group conflict has been virtually non-existent. There seem to be plenty of cargo ships to go around.

Pirate money certainly passes back and forth across international borders, but this movement is not necessarily extralegal. The Somali diaspora is one of the most interconnected and interdependent in the world, and the international exchange of funds should be viewed as family finances, rather than the monetary trail of a transnational criminal cartel.

MYTH #4: PIRATE GROUPS EMPLOY HIGHLY SOPHISTICATED INTELLIGENCE NETWORKS

Accompanying the claims of transnational pirate crime networks have been numerous media reports suggesting that pirate organizations are being fed vital shipping data enabling them to pick and choose targets from the tens of thousands of vessels charting the Indian Ocean and Gulf of Aden each year. In May 2009, for instance, Spanish media cited a European military intelligence report claiming that pirates were targeting specific ships identified by a team of "well-placed advisers" in London. "These consultants," the report read, "are in constant satellite telephone contact with pirate commanders on land, who can then pass details of the layout of the vessel, its crew, route and cargo to their colleagues at sea." The article went on to insinuate that the passing of such information, if true, represented a major intelligence failure on the part of the UK government: "It was unclear why leaks of such sensitive details appear to be coming from Britain."[7]

In reality, these so-called sensitive details are practically public knowledge, available to anyone with an Internet connection and access to an online maritime tracking service, such as Lloyd's Marine Intelligence Unit. By paying a subscription fee, users—such as these hypothetical "consultants"—are able to continually monitor the course and position of virtually any commercial shipping vessel in the world, as well as its cargo, crew manifest, and other details of interest to pirates (such as freeboard and maximum speed). But it is not clear that such information would be particularly useful; even with access to a maritime tracking service, intercepting a vessel on the open sea is not nearly as easy as it may seem. For security reasons, the vessels' exact coordinates are delayed by at least five or six hours, and plotting an intercept course using the commercially available GPS device a pirate attack group is likely to possess is an extremely formidable task. Even missing a pre-selected target by as little as half an hour would put a vessel moving at ten knots out of visual range, exposing its now-aimless pursuers to an increased risk of being picked up by international naval patrols, or even dehydration, starvation, and death. In myopically chasing a single target, moreover, the pirates would probably have to pass over a host of other perfectly suitable ships.

Roger Middleton voiced his own reasons for rejecting the existence of a sophisticated pirate intelligence network: "Why on earth would you need intelligence to hijack a ship in the Gulf of Aden? Spend half an hour googling and you can find where the shipping lanes are and therefore where the best targets are likely to be. You go north, and maybe left a little bit, and then you just wait." Middleton conceded that the vast Indian Ocean presented them with a greater navigational challenge, but argued that their basic strategy had remained unchanged. "If there were a certain ship sailing through the Indian Ocean and you wanted to catch it, then of course you'd need intelligence. But that's not the nature of this crime . . . it's not an intelligence-led crime—it's opportunistic. It's like walking down the street looking through windows: you see one that has a single glazing, so you smash the window, go in, and steal the TV."

The major hijackings hitting the news are bound to create the impression that pirate gangs purposefully go after only the juiciest of targets. But of the over two hundred vessels to have been successfully hijacked, only five—four oil supertankers and the tank transport MV *Faina*—could be considered "ideal targets." For the average pirate—ragged, ill-equipped, and often without enough food and fuel to get him home—any ship that floats is a welcome oasis in the desert.

MYTH #5: PIRATE DOLLARS ARE FUELLING A PROPERTY BOOM IN NAIROBI

The Nairobi suburb of Eastleigh, unofficially known as "Little Mogadishu," is a slice of Somalia transported into Kenya; the roads are unpaved and perpetually clogged with noisy traffic, and khat leaves litter the ground between colourful rows of open-air kiosks. As he dropped me off at the outskirts of the sprawling neighbourhood, my Kenyan taxi driver earnestly cautioned me to stay alert. "Somalis don't argue with you," he warned. "They just stab you."

House prices in Nairobi have risen two- and threefold over the last five years, and angry local residents have naturally turned to Somalis—already viewed with suspicion by native Kenyans—as convenient scapegoats. Since the piracy outbreak two years ago, the scapegoating has included allegations that pirate dollars are in large part responsible for the rising costs.[8] A few days earlier, a University of Nairobi medical student I had met on the streets downtown echoed the concerns felt by many Nairobi residents. "Somalis are buying all the land from the Kenyans," he exclaimed. "How? Where do they get all the money?"

Strolling down the streets of Eastleigh in December 2009, I could not deny that the neighbourhood was in the midst of a building boom. Alongside the broad thoroughfares carving up the suburb, layers of scaffolding snaked around the shells of six-storey buildings under construction. I stopped and began to question passers-by, and soon a small mob had gathered around me. I asked the crowd for their thoughts on a recent broadcast by the Kenyan Television Network, which had sent a team to Eastleigh with the express purpose of looking for pirates. "All they found were Toyota Surfs and *mirra* [the Kenyan term for khat]," one man shouted out. "That's not enough evidence!"

Irrespective of whether pirates are hiding out in Eastleigh, a rough calculation is sufficient to dismiss the notion that piracy has had anything to do with the skyrocketing demand for Nairobi land. At the time, pirate ransoms had not totalled more than $125 million; given how much pirate booty is blown on cars and khat, it would be a miracle if as much as a tenth had made its way from Somalia into the Nairobi property market. And $12.5 million in over two years could not noticeably affect average property prices in even the smallest slum of a global city like Nairobi.

Though admittedly not as glamorous an explanation, the Nairobi property boom has been a result of the Kenyan government's investor-friendly policies over the last half-decade—not the laundered proceeds of pirate kingpins.

* * *

Looking beyond the mythology that has coloured the reality of piracy both past and present, there are some striking similarities. Despite their notorious reputations, the pirates of old, like Somali pirates today, usually left their hostages alive (after all, they needed to provide an incentive for crews to surrender without a fight). Like

the Somalis, they were spendthrift; Captain Kidd was the only pirate known to have buried treasure, and he did not do so very often
(pirates didn't—and still don't—plan for the future). Even in their
organizational cultures, the two groups are remarkably similar; like
the Somalis, pirate crews on seventeenth-century vessels more resembled associations of shareholders than servants indentured to a
despotic captain.

Among the Somali pirates, of course, not all shareholders were
equal.

4

Of Pirates, Coast Guards, and Fishermen

THE DAY AFTER MY FARM MEETING WITH BOYAH, I WAS SITTING at the dining-room table of my guest house in Garowe, sipping a cup of Shah (sweet tea) and waiting for Abdirizak, my host and interpreter, to bring me a pirate. Before long, I heard Abdi's station wagon pulling through the fortified iron gate and into the courtyard, and he soon appeared with a sullen youth in tow. Consistent with the Somali nickname culture, Abdi introduced him as Ombaali, meaning "the burdened camel"; I learned only later that his real name was Abdulkhadar.

After interviewing a man considered by many to be the father of piracy in Puntland, I was speaking with one of its unknown sons. Over the course of three hijacking operations, Ombaali had served as one of Boyah's foot soldiers; he was a "holder," a low-ranking member of the group brought on board to guard the crew once the vessel had been captured and taken to harbour. Or so he claimed; when I later asked Boyah about Ombaali, he waved his hand dismissively and denied ever employing him.

Ombaali, though only in his mid-twenties, had crooked and rotten teeth, perpetually bared in a leering grin, and his eyes were bloodshot. His hunched frame, petite and almost childlike, barely filled out the standard combat fatigues of a Somali militiaman. A former truck driver, Ombaali had grown up in a poor inland village,

Hasballe, that lies in the corridor running from Garowe to Eyl, inhabited by the Isse Mahamoud sub-clan of Boyah and the gang's other Eyl-born leaders.

Ombaali seemed able to remember scant details of his pirating career. He claimed that the three ships on which he had served were hijacked sometime in 2008, though his most precise guess was that they were taken during "the early months of the year." The only other facts he was able to recall were the nationalities of two of the ships—Japanese and Yemeni—and, not surprisingly, the exact ransom amounts.

"We got $1.8 million for the Japanese tanker," he said, of a vessel carrying a cargo of crude oil. "And $1.6 million for the other one." The owners of the smaller Yemeni ship, on the other hand, did not deem the vessel or her crew to be worth ransoming, and in the end the gang simply let it go. Checking up on his story afterwards, I discovered only one vessel captured in 2008 that matched Ombaali's description: the MT *Stolt Valor*, a Japanese-owned chemical tanker hijacked in the Gulf of Aden while transporting oil products. Although the ransom paid to release the ship—reported to be between $1 million and $2.5 million—fits Ombaali's account, the *Stolt Valor* was seized on September 15, hardly "the early months of the year."

Ombaali paused to take a pinch of sugar from the bowl in the middle of the table, casually depositing it into his mouth. I hurriedly offered him some tea for the second time, but he shook his head, seeming surprised at my solicitude.

There were fifty individuals in his gang, he said, of whom fifteen were "attackers"—those who carried out the hijacking—and the remaining thirty-five were holders, such as himself. Ombaali differed slightly from Boyah in his account of how ransoms had been divided, telling me that 50 per cent was split amongst the attackers, 30 per cent went to the investors, and the remaining 20 per cent to the holders; unlike Boyah, Ombaali had no recollection of any money going to charity. Given that an attacker earned almost six times as much as a holder, I asked Ombaali why he had been content to settle for a blue-collar position.

"There is a management board, run by Boyah and others, that selects the attackers," he explained, presumably a reference to Boyah's Central Committee. "If I had stayed with the group, eventually I would have become an attacker."

Eight of the group's attackers, said Ombaali, had previous histories with the Somali-Canadian Coast Guard (SomCan), a private security firm that provided coast guard services to the Puntland government from 2002 to 2005, and again in 2008. "They were the most experienced at attacking and capturing," said Ombaali. They were probably also the most expert at marine navigation, including the operation of global positioning systems and other equipment. "GPS was very important," Ombaali confirmed. "We would never launch an operation without one."

The group had an interpreter, a Mogadishan named Yusuf, who had the dual responsibility of communicating with the crew as well as handling the ransom negotiation with the shipping company. Before working with Ombaali's group, Yusuf had been involved with a much more nefarious hijacking—though the case is perhaps better described as a kidnapping at sea. On June 23, 2008, pirates belonging to the northern Warsangali clan seized the German sailing yacht *Rockall* in the Gulf of Aden and brought it to the fishing town of Las Qoray, whereupon the middle-aged couple on board were taken ashore and force-marched into the mountains of Sanaag region. After being held for fifty-two days, during which they were allegedly abused and brutally beaten by the pirates, the Germans were released for a reported ransom of $1 million.[1] Yusuf's references from his previous employers must have been laudatory, because Ombaali's gang quickly sought his services. "We knew him from that operation, so we gave him a call," said Ombaali.

Interpreters, I would later learn, are in such high demand that they essentially functioned as independent contractors, hiring themselves out to various pirate groups and moving from job to job. Many translators are simply English-speaking members of the Somali diaspora out to make a few quick dollars in their homeland—where English is rarely spoken by the local inhabitants—while others establish themselves as *dilals*, professional negotiators who take pride in exacting the best possible price from shipowners.

From his two operations, said Ombaali, he had received a total of $50,000.[2] Unlike some of his more spendthrift colleagues—who had blown their earnings on cars and khat—Ombaali had invested in his future, using a portion of his profits to construct a house. "The rest I invested in a pirate operation," he said. "But I got unlucky. They were at sea for a long time, but they didn't find any ships."

Whatever Boyah's actual level of control over the day-to-day operations of the gang, Ombaali's testimony made it clear that the position of investor was open to anyone who had the money. Like many pirate operations, Boyah's extended group apparently employed a shareholder structure, with Boyah and the other members of the "management board" responsible for gathering funding from local investors and organizing the crew.[3]

With his dreams of early retirement dashed, Ombaali was forced back to work, albeit in the public sector; with his sub-clan, the Isse Mahamoud, now in power, he had had little difficulty in finding a job with the Puntland armed forces. If Ombaali was to be believed, this opportunity might have prevented his foray into the pirate world. "The reason that I became a pirate was that the government was not functioning," he said. "With the new government, I have expectations that things will change. If they do, I will stay a soldier. If not, I'll go back to the pirates."

Ombaali was evidently still struggling with this dilemma when I returned to Puntland five months later. By that time, he was working as a driver and bodyguard for Omar, one of my interpreters. When Omar fired him for incompetence, Ombaali repeatedly threatened to return to piracy unless he was reinstated. Following the failure of this strategy, Ombaali somehow got hold of my phone number, and would call me up to three times a day for no apparent reason.

Throughout the interview, Ombaali had sat squirming in his chair, his manner suggesting more the subject of a police interrogation than a friendly exchange. By the forty-minute mark I had clearly nearly exhausted his limited supply of patience, and he began to grumble about being late for an appointment. I squeezed in one final question: With hours of idle time and few diversions, how did he and his fellow guards get along with their hostages?

"We gave them the best treatment," he said. "We never stole anything from them, even their cellphones."

"But what if you had not received any ransom money?" I asked.

Ombaali leaned back in his chair and calmly replied, "Then we would have killed them all."

* * *

The decision to kill, thankfully, was not in Ombaali's hands, but in those of his fishermen bosses—the long-serving generals of the Central Committee, most of whom, years earlier, had begun the struggle against foreign incursions into their fishing waters. Since the foreign destruction of Somali fisheries is commonly cited as the impetus for piracy, it may be surprising to discover that fishing has never played much of a role in Somalia, either as a means of sustenance or as a sector in the formal economy.[4] In fact, prior to the 1970s virtually no Somalis engaged in fishing as a livelihood, and it was traditionally viewed as a somewhat ignoble occupation.

Like any good Marxist dictator, Mohamed Siad Barre sought to re-engineer his country's society and patterns of life. Aiming to reduce the population's overreliance on livestock, Siad Barre attempted to alter cultural attitudes about the value of fish, even going so far as to broadcast daily educational jingles over the radio exhorting nomads to "eat fish and make profit from it."[5] Natural disaster afforded him a more direct means of getting his message across; following severe droughts in 1974 and 1986, Siad Barre forcibly resettled tens of thousands of nomads into coastal towns, which soon developed into fishing communities.

In 1999, in response to persistent complaints from these communities about foreign fishing, Puntland president Abdullahi Yusuf brought in the British private security firm Hart Security to supply coast guard services to the nascent state. Yusuf did not contract Hart directly, but instead used an umbrella organization of local businessmen, the rapidly formed Puntland International Development Corporation. One of these intermediaries was Khalif Isse Mudan, a hotel proprietor and major shareholder in Golis Telecom, Puntland's largest mobile phone company. In February 2009, I met with Mudan in the office of the hotel he owned on the outskirts of Bossaso.

Working as partners, said Mudan, the Puntland government provided the coast guard's single ship and weaponry, with Hart Security responsible for the selection and training of its marine force. For the task of patrolling the sixteen-hundred-kilometre coastline of Puntland, Hart was given one twenty-metre trawler and a multi-clan force of seventy local men, armed with two aging ZU-23 Soviet anti-aircraft guns—weaponry on a par with that which the more prudent foreign fishing trawlers had begun to carry.

Hart Security's principal duty was to prevent illegal, unregulated, and unreported fishing in Puntland waters, and its operations were funded by selling official government fishing licences, issued through the Puntland Ministry of Fisheries, Ports, and Marine Transport. The licensing revenues were collected by Hart and split almost evenly with the government, the latter taking a 51 per cent share. "They were like joint venture investors," explained Mudan. For a fragile natural resource like the fisheries, a for-profit approach to licensing had obvious implications; the success of Hart's operation was defined not by the tranquillity of the waters it patrolled, but by the profits it generated, which in turn depended on the number of licences issued. The Ministry of Fisheries lent only a thin veneer of lawfulness to the process, as it had no policy in place to regulate the issuing of licences—nor any reliable marine research on which to base such a policy.

Despite Hart's support for foreign fishing companies, Mudan insisted that neither the firm nor its clients had entered into confrontations with local fishermen. "It was a very smooth operation," he assured me. Only five or six licences had been sold to short-range trawlers, and these had strict restrictions that prevented them from coming in contact with locals. "The trawlers weren't allowed to use very small-mesh nets," said Mudan, "or to come within less than ten miles of the shore."

According to Mudan, Hart focused its patrols in the waters from Hafun to Hobyo, a stretch of about six hundred kilometres in which most illegal fishing occurred. But even this reduced range consisted of a length of coastline greater than that running from Boston to New York, which Hart patrolled with one lone ship. In order to facilitate this immense job, the company set up observation posts in towns along the coast, from which it received daily reports via high-frequency radio, informing its forces of any suspicious ships fishing in the vicinity.

Hart's effectiveness was severely limited by the sheer territory its sole ship was tasked with patrolling. However, the company managed to arrest a number of foreign fishing vessels, most notably the Spanish fishing ship *Alabacora Quatro*, whose owner Hart successfully sued in a UK court, winning an undisclosed settlement.

Hart's patrols rarely brought its ship into contact with any pirates; the company's only significant encounter occurred in 2000, when the cargo vessel *Mad Express* was hijacked after experiencing technical problems near Bargaal. According to Hart chief Lord Richard Westbury, a former SAS officer, the pirates' level of sophistication was far below what they have demonstrated in recent years. "Basically, the pirates jumped off the ship. One injured his ankle," Westbury related in a January 2009 interview. "They certainly had no skills to operate in the way they are currently operating."[6]

* * *

Hart's operations in Puntland continued until 2002, when the company was unwillingly squeezed out of the business by the sudden arrival of the Somali-Canadian Coast Guard (SomCan), a private security firm headed by a former Toronto taxi driver named Abdiweli Ali Taar. The circumstances under which SomCan ousted Hart were decidedly suspicious. After the Puntland presidential election of 2001, which resulted in the victory of challenger Jama Ali Jama, the incumbent Abdullahi Yusuf attempted to oust Jama in a military coup. During the ensuing civil conflict from 2001 to 2002, the Ali Taar family—who belonged to the same Omar Mahamoud sub-clan as Yusuf—supported the former warlord in his fight against Jama. When Yusuf prevailed, the Ali Taars began operations in Puntland's waters. The brief civil war had also played itself out within the ranks of Hart's multi-clan coast guard force, which split into opposing factions; when fighting broke out near Hart's bases of operation, the firm packed up and set sail for the United Kingdom.[7]

A few days after speaking with Mudan, I met with two of SomCan's top executives, Said Orey and Abdirahman Ali Taar (elder brother of Abdiweli), on the patio of the same hotel. Joining us was Captain Abdirashid Abdirahim Ishmael, the commander of SomCan's marine forces.

Said Orey was quick to provide me with his no doubt partial explanation for Hart's hurried exit from Somalia. "Hart Security failed in its task," he claimed. "They weren't interested in the job. Hart failed to bring in sufficient equipment to properly protect the coast, and so people wanted a local company to do the job."

Though run by Somalis, the company did not represent much of a break from the past, being yet another private venture. SomCan seamlessly continued Hart's coast guard fishing licence business model, on an even greater scale. During its glory days, from 2002 to 2005, SomCan boasted an armada of six patrol boats and a force of four hundred marines, and claimed to have identified and arrested a total of thirty illegal fishing vessels. During this period, the company was heavily involved in selling fishing permits, with a quarterly licence fetching about $50,000. In some cases, the company was alleged to have bypassed the Ministry of Fisheries and issued fishing licenses directly to foreign concessions.

"Some licences were coming from the ministry," Mudan had told me a few days earlier, "and some were issued by SomCan itself. I saw one of them, in Dubai. And it was not issued by the ministry; it was signed by Abdiweli Ali Taar."

Puntland specialist Stig Jarle Hansen, who has conducted extensive research into the use of private security in the region, agreed. "As I understand it, Abdiweli Ali Taar was authorized to sell licences," he told me. "They were sold through networks, but SomCan was in the end responsible."

Unlike Hart, SomCan required foreign fishing companies to obtain a Somali agent to represent them. Once the companies— mostly Korean, Thai, or Japanese concerns—had established ties with a Somali businessman, local government militiamen would be placed on their ships to provide protection, particularly from hostile local fishermen. In many cases, the fishing companies also hired additional security through their Somali agents. "SomCan was keeping the security of their own licensed ships, instead of keeping the security of the sea," explained Abdiwahid Mahamed Hersi "Joaar," the long-serving director general of the Puntland Ministry of Fisheries, and an open critic of SomCan.

SomCan's tripartite role as law enforcer, trade commissioner, and independent contractor enabled the company to establish what could be described as a maritime protection racket. From 2002 to 2005, the coast guard served directly as an agent for the Thai concession Sirichai Fisheries, guaranteeing the company's security in Somali waters and protecting it from local fishermen-cum-pirates, even to the point of posting its own armed guards on the decks of Sirichai's ships. Sirichai's relationship with SomCan was literally skin tight; according to Noel Choong, director of the International Maritime Bureau's Piracy Reporting Centre, Sirichai went so far as to provide uniforms for the coast guard troops.[8]

If there was any conflict of interest in a government coast guard protecting a private client, it was lost on Orey. "Yes, we were the agent for Sirichai," he said. "It was always the best company at following the rules and regulations."

SomCan's penchant for defending a select group of foreign fishing ships ran directly counter to the coast guard's raison d'être and brought it into conflict with local fishermen. For this reason, said Orey, the Ministry of Fisheries kept a close eye on the activities of licensed ships. "There were always inspectors from the Ministry of Fisheries on-board ship, whose duty it was to check if they were using legal equipment, and to protect local fishing boats from them," he said. "Sometimes these ships would overrun small fishing boats, and the inspector's job was to stop them, to keep them away from the locals."

Despite these measures, confrontations were common. According to Hansen, SomCan actively defended both foreign and domestic "licensed" fishing vessels from local fishermen. "Local fishermen were often unable to obtain the proper permits," he said, "and were forcibly prevented from fishing by the coast guard." Exacerbating the problem was the fact that SomCan-licensed ships would routinely come within close range of the shore. "They were coming two miles from the shore. Several times they destroyed nets," Mudan had told me. "Foreign fishing ships came very close to the shore and local fishermen started firing on them. SomCan responded."

SomCan's first coast-guarding stint came to an inglorious end in March 2005, when its employees hijacked a fishing trawler operated by Sirichai Fisheries, the company's own client. In an incident that blurred the distinction between coast guards and pirates, three SomCan guards on board the fishing trawler *Sirichainava 12* seized control of the vessel, demanding an $800,000 ransom for its release. Their actions provoked a quick and decisive response; within hours, a joint British and American strike team freed the ship and took the renegades into custody. The US Navy subsequently transported them to Oman, after which they were brought to Thailand and sentenced to ten years' imprisonment for piracy. (The hijackers served only a few years of their prison term; in 2007, President Hersi arranged their release under unknown circumstances.)

What had prompted their ill-advised gamble was not completely clear. One report suggested that the hijacking was provoked by the non-payment of the guards' monthly $200 salary. Orey insisted that the men had been paid in full, but had simply gotten greedy.

In either case, the hijacking was an utter disaster for SomCan, costing the company its job with the Puntland government—at least temporarily.

*   *   *

SomCan received a second chance three years later. Two years after the company's dismissal, in 2007, the Saudi private security firm Al-Habiibi briefly assumed coast guard duties in Puntland, but was fired in February 2008 for refusing an order to liberate the hijacked Russian tugboat *Svitzer Korsakov*. Then-president General Mohamud Muse Hersi turned back to SomCan, which was more willing than Al-Habiibi to serve as pirate hunters.

From between the pages of his daily planner, Orey produced a folded copy of SomCan's current employment contract, signed with Hersi's government in July 2008. As had been the case with Hart, all licensing and fine revenues were to be split 51 per cent–49 per cent, with the Puntland government responsible for supplying the coast guard's ships, weapons, and equipment.

In recent days, the pirates had been presenting a challenge not seen during SomCan's previous coast-guarding tour, but Orey was confident that his company was ready. "It is over the last eight months that we have done our best work," he said. In October 2008, for example, SomCan had mounted a successful operation to liberate the hijacked MV *Wail*, a Panamanian-registered bulk carrier containing a consignment of cement owned by a local Somali businessman. Captain Ishmael, who led the rescue operation, described how the SomCan flagship, flanked by its two speedboats, had surrounded the pirates and dispatched a negotiator to discuss the situation. As the speedboat carrying SomCan's envoy approached the hijacked transport, the pirates opened fire, killing the craft's operator. In the ensuing firefight, SomCan marines captured ten of the hijackers, sustaining one injury and minor damage to their ship.

SomCan's other encounters with pirates had been less bloody, and even more successful. Orey cited three naval assaults against hijacked fishing ships held near Hafun, which in each case resulted in the bandits abandoning the vessel and melting before SomCan's onslaught. The objects of these rescues were all local Somali or Yemeni vessels, which, according to Orey, the pirates had intended to use as long-range motherships.

Despite these successes, Orey was quick to acknowledge that SomCan had a long way to go. Although the company possessed three cast-off patrol boats obtained from the Japanese coast guard—as well as two speedboats—the cost of fuel usually limited it to deploying only a third of its "fleet." [9] The company operated no coastal radar tracking stations and did not employ satellite surveillance; the only intelligence it received was conveyed by radio or telephone. SomCan was, in effect, a "Dial-a-Coast-Guard," whose counter-piracy activities were limited to after-the-fact responses: either commando-style raids on captive vessels, or, if given timely tip-offs, anticipatory assaults on land.

Even setting aside the difficulties in response time, the SomCan patrol ship's armament rendered it run-of-the-mill competition for many of the illegal fishing vessels it was routinely tasked with observing and intercepting. A few weeks earlier, Orey had been personally supervising a routine patrol from Bossaso to Hafun. As the SomCan ship was returning to port, it came across four foreign fishing vessels in close proximity to one another, each armed with an anti-aircraft gun, which Orey sardonically described as "almost the exact same kind as ours. They saw the anti-aircraft guns on our deck," he said, "and that was enough. They opened fire." Outmatched, the SomCan crew had few options. "Of course we fled," said Orey, "there was no way we were ready to fight them." Fortunately, no one was injured or killed in the engagement.[10] But the incident illustrated that SomCan was in need of a more lethal deterrent than the "Coast Guard" lettering on its ships before it would be able to administer justice in Somalia's anarchic waters.

* * *

After the dissolutions of Hart and SomCan in 2002 and 2005, respectively, their employees melted like a tide into the coastline. As Ombaali's testimony suggests, some of them discovered that their nautical training had practical applications at the opposite end of the employment spectrum from law enforcement. In an October 2008 report by the British think tank Chatham House, Captain Colin Darch, skipper of the hijacked Russian tugboat *Svitzer Korsakov*, related that several of the vessel's captors had previously belonged to the Puntland Coast Guard. "One pirate called Ahmed told us he had been in the coast guard," he said, "and only Ahmed and one or two others who had also been coast guards understood our engines."[11]

The involvement of ex-Puntland Coast Guard marines in piracy is hardly surprising. The skills and experience possessed by former coast guards—trained to a European standard in sharpshooting, maritime navigation, and boarding and seizure operations—made them perfect employees for the new businesses springing up around the Gulf of Aden. The Somali pirates who burst onto the scene in 2007 and 2008 were organized to a level attested by the immediacy of their success, and by the millions of dollars that were literally airlifted their way. Long-range motherships and advanced navigation systems like GPS and radar made it possible for them to carry out deep-water operations. These technologies—as well as larger investments in fuel and weapons—extended the pirates' attack radius hundreds of kilometres from the coast. During the extended hunting trips into the wilderness of international waters that characterized this new wave of pirates, a former coast guard's knowledge of GPS systems, radar, and the more complex engines on board the mother-ships would be an invaluable asset.

* * *

The peaceful election of Abdirahman Farole—a PhD candidate from Melbourne's La Trobe University—in January 2009 was regarded as something of a landmark in Puntland politics; he was only the second civilian Somali leader, along with Somaliland founder Mo-hamed Egal, since the assassination of Somali Republic president Abdirashid Ali Shermarke in 1969. During his political campaign, Farole promised to get tough on piracy, a stance he has reiterated in media interviews since his election. Hoping to tease out the specif-ics of his plan, I spoke with him at the presidential compound in the centre of Garowe.

Farole, meaning "fused toes," was a nickname that the president had inherited from his great-grandfather. In his mid-sixties, Farole was diminutive, but the intensity of his almost-feline eyes com-manded an authority that his body did not; they seemed to swallow anyone meeting his gaze. The president was an erudite man, fluent in English, Arabic, and Italian, and his first sentence to me inaugur-ated a half-hour lecture on the history of Somalia's current tribula-tions; finally, I managed to steer the conversation towards the topic of the Puntland Coast Guard.

"We are nowhere near being able to establish a functioning coast guard," Farole began bluntly. "This force must be professionally trained and equipped with speedboats, telecommunications, and GPS technology, heavy weapons, and a continual supply of fuel," he said, at a cost that the Puntland government was unable to shoulder. With his administration struggling to keep up with monthly army wages of $30, financing the monthly coast guard salary of $300 (a necessary wage, said the president, for a highly skilled job requiring long periods spent absent from families) for a hundreds-strong force would be impossible without international financial assistance.

"Money will also be needed to reward marines who successfully capture pirate vessels," said Farole, adding that additional funds would be required to satisfy traditional Somali clan law, or *heer,* which requires compensation to be paid to the families of soldiers killed in action. Hearing the president speak, it was clear that he anticipated much blood being spilt—for him, a resolute and dogged fight against piracy would be a war, with casualties unavoidable. "Unless you truly get the will and commitment of the people behind you," said Farole, "you cannot win any war."

Winning a war also requires a command of logistics, an area in which the president admitted Puntland was notably deficient. The region possesses close to half of Somalia's thirty-three-hundred-kilometre coastline, yet communications, radar, and satellite centres in the Indian Ocean and the Gulf of Aden—which would provide intelligence and coordination to the coast guard—are yet to be established. Additionally, mechanisms are still required to integrate the Puntland Coast Guard with the institutions of NATO, the European Union, the International Maritime Bureau, and individual foreign navies.

The president had little faith in the ability of a private security firm to overcome these formidable challenges. When I asked about SomCan's future role as coast guard, his response was guardedly noncommittal—but not optimistic. "I don't believe they will be effective for this difficult task," he said. "Because they didn't do anything in the past." For the moment, at least, the president was not looking to hand over SomCan's job to anyone else once the company's present contract expired.

"We are not prepared to create a coast guard without international help," Farole said, adding that the fight against the pirates would be in the hands of Puntland's regular ground troops, deployed from their Bossaso garrison. For Farole, however, international concerns over piracy were of secondary importance to those closer to home. "Measures need to go beyond preventing piracy against commercial ships," he said. "Piracy is [the international community's] problem—well, it's ours too—but what is *specifically* our problem is illegal fishing." Until illegal fishing was curtailed, the president was adamant that the ministry's days as a licence printing press were over: "We are not planning to issue any fishing licences before we have full control of our seas."

The Puntland government's dream of gaining sovereignty over its seas remains distant. Puntland currently relies almost entirely on foreign warships to provide ersatz coast guard services in the Gulf of Aden and the Indian Ocean (only the day before I spoke with the president, the French navy had handed over nine Somali captives to Puntland officials—a far more tempered response than the overzealous Operation Thalathine). But operating an international armada at a cost of tens of millions per month is not sustainable; eventually, a locally owned coast guard, one free of Hart's and SomCan's unsavoury legacy of profiteering, will be required to safeguard Somalia's dangerous waters.

* * *

On June 30, 2009, SomCan's contract with the Puntland government expired, and—not surprisingly—was not renewed. During the last few months of its tenure, SomCan—perhaps still hoping to prove its worth to the new administration—continued to hunt illegal fishing ships with furious resolve. On March 12, the company's boat headed out of Bossaso harbour on patrol, and on March 31 it caught up with two ships fishing illegally near Hafun. After escorting them back to Bossaso and impounding them, the SomCan owners were greeted with an irate reaction from the Ministry of Fisheries, which produced copies of two licences that it had recently issued to the vessels (which were subsequently released). Apparently, just a few months after Farole had assured me of his government's intention to scrap the corrupt fishing licensing schemes of past Puntland administrations, the arbitrary issuing of licences had seamlessly resumed.

These developments were not welcomed by Said Orey, a fact he made clear on the porch of my Garowe residence shortly before the expiration of SomCan's contract. "We are entitled to collect 49 per cent of the proceeds of all fishing licences sold by the Puntland government, but the fishing ministry won't even tell us it's selling them," he said, looking disgusted. "It's clear that people from the Ministry of Fisheries are working with illegal fishing interests."

A few days later, over lunch at the house of a mutual friend, I asked Director General Joaar about the ministry's renewed interest in the licence-printing business. "Yes, we started selling licences again—with the permission of the president—for forty-five-day periods," he admitted. "But only six have been sold so far."

When I brought up SomCan's contractual right to almost half the revenue from the licences, Joaar waved his hand dismissively.

"Said Orey is himself a pirate," he declared, partly in jest. "Our office still hasn't received a copy of that contract. It was a deal that was completely under the table." Or so Joaar claimed.

SomCan and the Ministry of Fisheries butted heads for a second time towards the end of May, after the company attacked and arrested three more foreign fishing vessels in the vicinity of Bargaal. These vessels, according to Orey, were entirely different from the two arrested in the March incident, but Joaar insisted that two of the three were the exact same ships SomCan had erroneously captured two months earlier. "This time, I told them: 'If you think you can capture those ships, go ahead and try—because they have security on board,'" said Joaar. This security had been provided by the Puntland government after the vessel's previous run-in with SomCan, as Joaar freely admitted. "If we give them licences," he explained, "we are responsible for what happens to them."

The SomCan patrol ship had nonetheless confronted the vessels, and, after they refused to surrender, opened fire. Responding to the fishing vessels' distress calls, the Spanish warship *Numancia*, the flagship of the European Union fleet, arrived and attempted to mediate the situation. After receiving confirmation from unidentified onshore ministry officials—relayed through the *Numancia*—that the ships were legally licensed, SomCan disengaged and left the scene. Following the episode, Orey told me, he received a personal rebuke from the office of the president.

At best, these incidents revealed a buffoonish lack of coordination between the Puntland government and its supposed official coast guard; at worst, an endemic state of venality and double-dealing within the Puntland Ministry of Fisheries that had been granted President Farole's blessing. In any case, the ministry's—and Joaar's—antipathy towards SomCan seemed somewhat self-defeating: without a coast guard backing it up, one wonders why any foreign fishing vessel would ever bother to buy a Puntland licence. But the potential loss of revenue did not seem to dampen Joaar's sense of triumph over his adversaries.

"SomCan is finished," he said, wiping his hands together. "No more."

* * *

SomCan's demise, however, did not bring an end to the Puntland government's dalliances with private security contractors. In November 2010, Puntland entered into a deal with Saracen International, a South African private security firm with no clear address, to "train and mentor" a "Puntland Marine Force." [12] Even by the standards of the murky Hart and SomCan deals, Puntland's agreement with Saracen had all the transparency of a muddy lake. The firm—whose Ugandan subsidiary has been fingered by the UN Security Council for training rebel paramilitary forces in the Congo—is headed by Lafras Lutingh, a former officer in the Civil Cooperation Bureau, a notorious apartheid-era internal security force. [13] Several months after the announcement of the Puntland deal, Saracen was revealed to be covertly backed by Erik Prince, founder of Blackwater (now

Xe Services), the much-maligned military contractor implicated in the 2007 deaths of fourteen Iraqi civilians. Saracen is currently in the process of training a one-thousand-strong anti-piracy militia in Puntland, equipped with 120 pickup trucks, four armoured vehicles, and six patrol aircraft.[14] The funding for this ambitious program, Somali officials initially announced, would come from an unnamed Middle Eastern country (later revealed to be the United Arab Emirates) with a vested commercial interest in keeping the Gulf of Aden shipping lane pirate-free. Under intense pressure from the United Nations and other international actors, who slammed the venture for violating the UN arms embargo on Somalia, Saracen was forced to fold the operation.

It is an open question whether the Puntland Marine Force would have fared better than its ill-fated predecessors. Far from being an impartial government actor, the coast guard operated as a business enterprise, generating its own revenues through the sordid sale of fishing permits to private clients. Instead of preventing violent confrontations between the locals and foreign fishing fleets, the coast guard took sides, posting armed guards on the decks of a select group of foreign vessels. In doing so, it accentuated the grievances that were driving the local fishermen to commit feats of piracy.

After doing its bit to effectively accelerate the rise of piracy in Puntland, in 2005 the SomCan Coast Guard fell from grace when rogue employees themselves took a turn at hijacking. When the company subsequently dispersed, many of its former employees, trained to *combat* piracy, themselves joined the burgeoning ranks of pirates sweeping into the Gulf of Aden. In early 2009, SomCan completed the circuit, actively recruiting so-called "reformed pirates" into its ranks.

First in line was one of Eyl's most notorious sons, the infamous Garaad Mohammed.

5

Garaad

IN THE EVER-SHIFTING WORLD OF PIRATES, COAST GUARDS, AND fishermen, the movement amongst the three professions has never been in only one direction. As some coast guards have transitioned to piracy, so have some pirates made the shift into coast-guarding. Of this latter trend, there is no better example than Garaad Mohammed.

Like many pirate pioneers, Garaad grew up as a fisherman in Eyl, joining his comrades in the struggle against illegal fishing. Beginning in 2003, Garaad, along with Boyah and the other Eyl veterans, travelled south to Harardheere to provide training to Afweyne's Somali Marines. Garaad's bloodline made him an ideal inter-clan go-between; his father belonged to the Isse Mahamoud of Eyl, but his mother was born Habir Gedir, the same sub-clan as Afweyne and the other Harardheere pirates.

Shortly after he began joint operations with the Marines, Garaad founded his own group, the National Volunteer Coast Guard (NVCG), an organization based in the southern city of Kismaayo that specialized in targeting small boats and fishing vessels. But even after the formation of the NVCG, Garaad's affiliation with Afweyne and the Harardheere gangs did not end, and he continued to finance gangs operating out of central and northern Somalia.

On April 8, 2009, four of Garaad's henchmen, operating from the commandeered Taiwanese fishing vessel *Win Far 161*, attacked the MV *Maersk Alabama* several hundred kilometres off the central Somali coast as she was steaming towards Mombasa. In what was the first piracy of a US-registered vessel in two centuries, the hijackers boarded the vessel and took Captain Richard Phillips and two other American citizens hostage on the bridge. As the leader of the attackers attempted to locate the rest of the crew, he was ambushed in the darkened engine room by the *Alabama*'s chief engineer, Mike Perry, who, though armed only with a knife, managed to overpower him. After the leader was released in a bungled attempt to exchange him for Captain Phillips, all four hijackers fled in the *Alabama*'s cramped lifeboat, taking Phillips along with them.

The destroyer USS *Bainbridge* was the first US warship to arrive at the scene, as if guided by the spirit of her namesake, Commodore William Bainbridge, a nineteenth-century naval officer who had played a pivotal role in the war against the Barbary pirates of northern Africa. A tense hostage standoff with the lifeboat ensued. Over the next three days, the increasingly jittery pirates—whom Phillips nicknamed "The Leader," "Musso," "Tall Guy," and "Young Guy"—subjected him to sadistic psychological torture, the details of which Phillips related in a book about the incident, *A Captain's Duty:*

> "When we kill you, we're going to put you in an unclean place," the Leader said. "That's where I'm taking you now."
>
> "What does that mean?"
>
> They explained that they knew about this shallow reef where the water was stagnant. It wasn't part of a tide pool that came in and washed the bay every twelve hours. Any body dropped there would rot and bloat and stink to high heaven.
>
> "Very bad place," Musso said.
>
> I couldn't hold it any longer. I felt a rush of wetness on my pant leg. They were letting me piss myself like a goddamn animal.
>
> The rage just welled up in me. I felt degraded. I was screaming at the pirates, just cursing them and telling them they were going to die.[1]

For three of the four men, Phillips's morbid prediction came true. On April 12, believing Phillips's life to be in immediate danger, Commander Frank Castellano ordered the *Bainbridge* forces into action, upon which Navy SEAL snipers killed the three hijackers remaining on the lifeboat. The Leader, Abdiweli Muse (a Puntlander from Galkayo), who had been on board the *Bainbridge* conducting ransom negotiations when the rescue took place, suddenly found his bargaining position shot to bits. He was taken to New York to stand trial, and in February 2011 was sentenced to almost thirty-four years in prison.

Following the *Alabama* attack, Garaad vowed revenge against the Americans, and ordered his organization to retaliate. Two days later, a boatload of Garaad's men sighted the MV *Liberty Sun*, a US-flagged vessel carrying food aid destined for Somalia, which they proceeded to pursue and blast with rocket-propelled grenades; fortunately, neither the vessel nor her crew were harmed. In a subsequent phone interview with the Agence France-Presse, Garaad made it clear that the motive for the attack was anything but financial. "We were not after a ransom," he said. "We . . . assigned a team with special equipment to chase and destroy any ship flying the American flag in retaliation for the brutal killing of our friends."[2]

In February 2009, two months before the *Alabama* hijacking, I had sat across a table from Garaad on the patio of a Bossaso hotel, listening to him discuss his plans to join the Puntland Coast Guard.

* * *

I had been trying to get in touch with him for weeks, but Garaad had exhibited a tendency to disappear for long stretches of time once the initial contact was made. My interpreter Warsame and I had been supposed to meet him the previous day, but after preliminary discussions in the morning, Garaad turned off his phone and we didn't hear back from him. "He's off chewing khat somewhere," Warsame suggested. The next day, Garaad called us with his explanation: "I was busy."

After agreeing to meet us at four o'clock, his phone was off again. It was twenty minutes past four, and I was starting to get worried. I had heard disturbing reports of Garaad's lack of regard for conventional notions of politeness; one of my hosts, Abdirizak, recounted how Garaad had stood him up for a 10 a.m. meeting two days in a row. When one of our party informed Warsame and me that he had recently spotted Garaad near the khat market, chewing with some friends, it seemed that today's rendezvous was destined to share a similar fate. "Forget it," said Warsame, "he's not coming. He won't move for the rest of the afternoon." Soon afterwards, we got a call; despite the hypnotic powers of the khat, Garaad was on his way to the hotel. "His phone must have been off to avoid the people calling him for money," our friend suggested.

At about twenty-five minutes past four, Garaad showed up at the gated entrance to the hotel, and Warsame and I joined him on the restaurant patio. With his freshly ironed dress shirt, pressed slacks, and clean, cropped hair, Garaad blended right in with the crowd of Somali businessmen staying at the hotel. In contrast to his impeccable outfit, his face looked ragged and exhausted for someone in his mid-thirties, his eyes scratched raw by the constant rubbing of his fingers—a textbook case of khat withdrawal. Like Boyah, his face was slightly emaciated, and Warsame suggested afterwards that, like Boyah, he may have also been suffering from tuberculosis—perhaps indicative of a pirate-specific strain of the disease making the rounds. Also like Boyah, the indifference he showed towards me bordered on disdain. He shook my hand with a limp and lifeless motion, barely glancing in my direction. Throughout our meeting, he continually checked his phone, peering around as if hoping for someone to come and take him to the real interview.

Like "Butch Cassidy" or "Billy the Kid," "Garaad" was an outlaw sobriquet that had grown notorious in its own time—at least within the borders of Puntland. Like most pirate handles, his was an assumed name, taken from the Somali word for "clan elder," and was thus a sign of his status amongst his colleagues. In the world of Somali seafaring careers, Garaad had scaled the corporate ladder with remarkable dexterity, rising from artisanal fisherman to fishing vessel hijacker, and finally to one of the most famous pirate organizers and financiers in Puntland.

As I began my questions, Garaad instantly prickled when he heard the word "pirate."

"Illegal fishing ships, they are the real pirates," he rejoined. "I don't know where they all come from, but there are nearly five thousand ships doing illegal fishing in our territory." Garaad's estimate, far more generous than the 200–250 illegal ships projected by the Puntland Ministry of Fisheries, may have been coloured by his strong personal sentiments.

"I was one of the first to start fighting against the illegal fishing, before Boyah," he bristled. So far, his quest against the "real pirates" of Somalia had netted Garaad a total of about a dozen illegal fishing ships. Despite these successes, he assured me that little in the way of ransom money has come his way. "Ransom negotiations over captured fishing ships are very difficult," he said, "because the people you're dealing with . . . drag the negotiations on and on. They don't care how long you keep the ships, they won't pay you anything." But Garaad insisted that his goal was not to make money, but to fight illegal fishing. Aiding him in his crusade, he said, was a pirate army spanning the entire length of the Somali coast.

"I have direct control over a total of eight hundred hijackers operating in thirteen groups spread from Bossaso, through Hafun, Eyl, Harardheere, Hobyo, and Kismaayo," he said. Each of these groups had a "sub-lieutenant" who reported directly to Garaad and did not make a move without his authorization, he claimed. "Independent groups"—those whom he did not control—accounted for an additional eight hundred individuals. To take Garaad at his word, therefore, would have been to give him credit for exerting a half-Stalinist, half-Mafioso grip over half of Somalia's estimated 1,500–2,000 pirates, spread over a criminal empire stretching almost twenty-five hundred kilometres of lawless coastline. Given the decentralized nature of most pirate operations, it was an understatement to say that Garaad's self-portrayal stretched credulity thin.

"If the international community ever pays us our rightful compensation for the illegal fishing," he said, "attacks will stop within forty-eight hours." As to what this compensation might entail, Garaad was less than specific. "Nobody can count it," he answered. "It's a lot of money. The people of the world know how long they have been doing illegal fishing, and from that they can calculate how much they owe us."

*   *   *

Throughout our interview, Garaad seemed anxious to prove that he was no profiteer. His manner was evasive whenever I asked for specific monetary details, and persistent questioning invariably caused him to retreat. "I've never personally attacked commercial ships," he said. "The only one I've ever captured is the *Stella Maris*, and the reason for it was the financial problems we were having then. At the time, there was a lack of illegal fishing vessels to attack, and we needed money to keep our operations going."

The MV *Stella Maris*, a Japanese-owned bulk carrier, was seized in the Gulf of Aden in July 2008 and held for eleven weeks before being released for a ransom of $2 million, which Garaad reinvested in future operations. His operating expenses since then must have been rather high, because Garaad insisted that he was broke. "I don't have one cent," he said. "I don't even have a house."

Despite his protestations of poverty, the word was that Garaad had been involved with the hijacking of the MV *Faina*, the Ukrainian transport ship laden with Russian tanks that first drew international media attention to the Somali coast. But his level of involvement was anyone's guess, and Garaad himself was not going to provide any clarification. When I asked him about the *Faina*, he immediately tensed up, telling me that he "supported some young guys" for the mission, but volunteering no more information.

There is a credible rumour, however, surrounding Garaad's involvement. In December 2008, Garaad reportedly left Garowe with a cohort of armed men, aiming to relieve the *Faina* hijackers and bring them back to safety in Puntland. They were much in need of his assistance; after forcing the captured ship to anchor at Harardheere, south of the Puntland coast, the US Navy had proceeded to encircle and blockade the pirates on board the *Faina*. On shore, the environment was equally hostile; Harardheere was near territory controlled by the Islamist organization Al-Shabaab, and the group's militias were waiting patiently inland to relieve the *Faina* pirates of their ransom as soon as they dared come ashore.

Into this melee allegedly charged Garaad, his Toyota cavalry gleaming in the sun. His intention, presumably, was to escort the hijackers to Puntland once they had secured the ransom payment for the *Faina*. Unfortunately, on his way to Harardheere, Al-Shabaab militants reportedly ambushed Garaad's convoy, confiscated his weapons and vehicles, and left him, unharmed, to make the long journey back to Puntland on foot. At the first opportunity, I asked Garaad for the truth behind this incredible story. His shields instantly dropped. "No, that's not true, I wasn't involved with that," he said. "I don't have any enemies, only friends . . . everyone is happy with the job I'm doing."

After four months in captivity, the *Faina* had finally been released a week before our meeting, commanding a then-record bounty of $3.2 million. Considering that he had partially financed the mission, Garaad was curiously ignorant of the state of his investment. "I was busy with other things," he said. "I didn't hear about any ransom money." A few moments later, his memory seemed to clear up. "We didn't get that much money," he said. "By the time it finally came down to it, everyone only got a few thousand. A lot of money was spent on that ship, and hundreds of people were involved."

This is one part of Garaad's story, at least, that I was able to verify independently, through a Nairobi source who had been directly involved in the *Faina* ransom negotiation process. As the negotiation dragged on, my source told me, burgeoning expenses forced the original hijackers (Afweyne's group) to approach three or four additional pirate organizations for financial assistance—in effect, issuing stock in their operation. By the time the ransom was delivered, the complement on board the ship had ballooned to over a hundred pirates.

* * *

As the interview progressed, Garaad gradually began to open up.

"Right now, as I talk to you, there are twenty different groups I'm invested in, from Kismaayo to Hafun." He hesitated before continuing. "We control the entire Somali coast." When asked what he thought of Boyah's recent radio-announced ceasefire, a mocking note entered his voice as he shook his head. "My organization is different . . . We're not similar to Boyah . . . We are going to keep going until our seas are cleansed of illegal fishing ships."

When I asked for the names of some of the commercial ships seized by his organization, Garaad deflected my question once more. "I don't know the names of any of the ships my men capture, and I don't care," he said. "The only thing I care about is sending more pirates into the sea.

"Sometimes, the commercial vessels," he continued, "have the same names as the illegal fishing ships. They are owned by the same companies . . . so that makes it legal to capture those commercial ships as well."

Garaad's tenuous justification sounded similar to the Roman emperor Caligula's remark upon being told that he had executed the wrong man for a crime: "That one deserved it just as much." Fishing companies and international shippers rarely share parent companies, but to Garaad, any ship he caught merited equal punishment.

Garaad's vehement quest for maritime justice had recently brought him into the open arms of SomCan, which at the time still had four months remaining on its contract. "Yes, I will be part of

[SomCan]," he said. "If the coast guard is going to stop people from doing illegal fishing, destroying the marine environment, and doing toxic dumping, then we will work with them." In other words, having tried his hand at fishing and piracy, Garaad was looking for a shot at coast-guarding. "The reason I'm with SomCan now," Garaad said, "is because they have special ships that are well-armed with proper guns—with anti-aircraft guns—and their ships are capable of getting close to the illegal fishers." Pressed for specifics about his job description, he continued, "I will be training their marines, and providing them with information and intelligence."

Given his adamant hatred of illegal fishing, Garaad was curiously unconcerned by the fact that his current partners had only recently been in the business of protecting the very foreign ships he vowed to hunt down. "The reason I joined them," Garaad said, "is that they told me that they stopped those practices. If I see that they are still doing that, then we'll have a problem."

As a "reformed pirate," Garaad hoped to be a kind of Hannibal Lecter of Puntland, helping the authorities hunt down the serial hijackers of the Gulf of Aden. But "reformed" might have been a premature descriptor, for Garaad was not about to give up his pirate activities just because he happened to be working as a coast guard. "The agreement I made is to help them fight against illegal fishing," he said. "These days, I'm concentrating on illegal fishing ships. But I will still be doing my other operations on the side."

The exact nature of Garaad's coast-guarding aspirations seemed to vacillate. In one version, his aim was to serve SomCan in a capacity falling somewhere between naval school drill instructor and marine commando; in another, he would use his supposedly massive pirate empire as a paramilitary force to fight foreign fishing in Somali waters, with SomCan tagging along for the ride. His next statement appeared to support this latter interpretation. "SomCan is one of us now," he said, "it is part of our organization." Garaad would not give any more details of the terms of his agreement, other than to say that it would remain in effect as long as illegal fishers trawled

Somali seas. Despite our lengthy exchange, it was impossible to say what he saw as his role in SomCan, and I was beginning to think he had little idea himself.

Hoping to clarify these ambiguities, I brought up the subject of Garaad's employment during my meeting with the SomCan executives the following day. I quickly learned an interesting fact: Garaad was the cousin of SomCan co-owner Said Orey. "Yes," said Orey, "we've been in contact with Garaad. As his relative, it is my duty to stop him from doing bad things." Garaad's role in the company, Orey was quick to emphasize, would be to work on board ship as a marine, "not as a coast guard trainer."

Hiring a pirate to police coastal waters seemed like hiring a bank robber to guard the vault, and, in Garaad's case, one who intended to keep robbing banks during his off-hours. Yet Garaad was not the only pirate SomCan was hoping to work with. What the company had in mind, Orey told me, was a kind of employment retraining program for pirates. "Let us first try and educate these young guys," Orey said, "and if we succeed, then, whoever refuses to cooperate, maybe we can fight against them." At SomCan's behest, Garaad was using his influence to recruit as many pirates as possible into its ranks. According to Orey, many were already lining up to get fitted for uniforms. Yet, if Garaad was any indication, transforming dozens of erstwhile pirates into marine security officers would be a difficult task, especially if many of them also saw their new job as fundamentally identical to their old one.

For better or worse, the end of SomCan's contract quashed its pirate employment experiment in its infancy. Garaad, however, appeared to have seen some limited service with the company before being decommissioned. According to Joaar, SomCan's May 2009 attack on the three ministry-licensed fishing vessels was carried out by a strike team composed of former pirates. "There were sixteen pirates from Eyl onboard, including Garaad," he said. "These [SomCan owners] are crazy people."

* * *

Our meeting over, Garaad got up and silently walked away. An hour after he left, a call came to Warsame's phone: it was Garaad, asking for his help to arrange an interview with President Farole. As with Boyah, his reason for talking to me had been rendered perfectly transparent.

He was, I heard, already back with his friends, chewing khat as the sun set.

6

Flower of Paradise

THE ARRIVAL OF KHAT IN GAROWE IS A CURIOUS SIGHT.

Each day at around noon, the first khat transports begin to roll in from Galkayo, coinciding with the typical waking hour for a pirate. The angry honking of the incoming vehicles rouses the city from its lethargy, bringing expectant crowds flocking into the streets in defiance of the midday heat. Screaming down the highway at reckless speeds, high beams flashing, guards perched on top, the transports arrive on the southern road. Turning off the highway and rumbling down the embankment towards Garowe's main checkpoint, they are eagerly greeted by barking soldiers, who fill their arms with leafy bundles before waving the vehicles through. Behind the barrier, a fleet of white station wagons stands ready to be loaded; hired hands follow behind female merchants decked in vibrant headdresses, hauling rectangular bushels wrapped in brown canvas.

As the transports arrive at the khat market, or *suq,* the whole city begins to buzz with activity. Throngs of shouting men press into the *suq* as older children and adolescents mob the transports, hoping to snatch what they can in the scramble of the unloading. In the poorer neighbourhoods, barefoot children gather in circles in front of hovels, slapping hands and jostling for a few stalks scattered in the dust. Even the goats respond with Pavlovian consistency to the tooting of the station wagons, trotting after them in the hopes of nabbing a few fallen leaves.

This is the most significant daily event in Garowe life, repeated with unfailing precision every single day of the year. Steadily increasing in popularity in recent years, khat has become—along with livestock and fishing—one of Puntland's most lucrative economic sectors. As a Puntland cabinet minister once told me: "In Somalia, there are two industries that work: *hawala* [money transfer] and khat." If so, piracy has certainly made the khat trade work even better—since late 2008, the *suq* has been awash with the freshly minted bills of pirate ransoms, threatening to turn a tolerable vice into a national addiction.

* * *

Across clime, culture, and continent, people will find some way to intoxicate themselves. In Somalia, a uniformly Islamic society where alcohol consumption is highly taboo, the intoxicant of choice is khat, an amphetamine-like stimulant consumed either by chewing the plant's leaves or by steeping its dried leaves to make a tea.

Khat—which the Arabs nicknamed the "flower of paradise"—has for centuries been used by Muslim scholars to assist the performance of their intensive day- and night-long studies (and, in more modern times, by Kenyan and Ethiopian students cramming for exams).[1] Growing up to twenty metres high, the plant is extremely water-intensive and better suited to altitudes of 1,500–2,500 metres, giving the Ethiopian highlands and the provinces of northern Kenya a strong natural advantage over Somalia. Once confined to East Africa, the demand for the drug has been globalized over the last twenty years by refugees from conflicts in Somalia and Ethiopia; facilitated by modern transportation technologies, khat can now readily be found on the streets of London, Amsterdam, Toronto, Chicago, and Sydney.[2]

A social drug, khat is usually chewed for hours on end by groups of friends in picnic-like settings. Owing to its bitter taste, it is often accompanied by a special, heavily sugared tea or other sweet beverage, such as 7-Up. Once harvested, the plant retains its potency for only a short time and must be consumed fresh—the plant's active chemical, cathinone, breaks down within forty-eight hours after its leaves have dried—a fact that explains its previous lack of international distribution. Shipments to Puntland are flown three times daily from Nairobi and Addis Ababa into Galkayo airport. As is often the case with products designated for export, the khat that finds its way into Garowe is reputed to be of the lowest quality.

One company, SOMEHT, is responsible for importing virtually all of Puntland's khat, around seven thousand kilograms per day as of 2006.[3] According to Fadumo—a Garowe khat merchant whom I interviewed—each plane is greeted at the airstrip by large numbers of independent distributors, who deploy a network of transports for the slow and bumpy 250-kilometre journey from Galkayo to Garowe. Such is the addiction inspired by this delectable plant that crowds of youth throw up improvised roadblocks composed of small rocks or metal drums at frequent intervals by the sides of the road. At these unofficial checkpoints the young men, often armed with Kalashnikovs, clamour for handouts of the shrub. The drivers are happy to mollify their dangerous fans, throwing offerings of khat out the window at the outstretched hands as they pass. On rare occasions, these self-appointed tax collectors become too persistent, and are shot at, and sometimes killed, by the security guards stationed atop the trucks. Nonetheless, the khat trade generates relatively little attendant violence; Fadumo had never heard of a shipment being hijacked.[4]

Once the transports arrive at the main checkpoint outside Garowe, individual merchants meet them and transfer the cargo to their own cars. Fadumo's arrangements were informal; she tended to buy from a regular distributor, but would sometimes go to other suppliers for smaller amounts, or if her supplier was out of stock.

Though khat has long been a facet of Somali life, the last decade has seen imports into the country soar, and Puntland's piracy explosion in late 2008 brought consumption levels onto a whole new plane. Outside of cars and khat, there is not much available in Puntland on which to spend tens of thousands of dollars, and pirates are famous for the almost religious fervour with which they chew the drug (though they seem to lack the corresponding devotion to Koranic study). So overblown is the pirates' infatuation with khat that at times it approaches comical proportions; there are stories, from the early days of multimillion-dollar ransoms, of recently paid pirates rushing to the khat *suq* and spending their US hundred-dollar bills as if they were thousand-shilling notes (which are worth about three cents).

Even without this absurd level of reckless spending, the money disappears remarkably quickly. A successful pirate is expected to share his good fortune with his friends and relatives; the moment he steps off the ship, his money begins to diffuse through an endless kinship network, ending only when the last of the khat leaves have been chewed up and spit out.

* * *

In its short-term effects, khat resembles its South American equivalent, the coca leaf, causing mild euphoria, heightened energy, garrulousness, and appetite loss. Another effect is the belief in one's own invincibility, which many Somalis view as a factor contributing to the endemic conflict plaguing their country; like pirates, Somali militants are renowned for their rampant khat use, and the drug is thought to help fuel the violence (albeit to a lesser degree than in Liberia, where warlords reputedly rubbed cocaine into the open wounds of their soldiers before sending them into battle).[5] As Jamal, my neighbour during the last leg of my flight into Somalia, eloquently explained, "When people chew khat they believe that they have superhuman strength. They would even think they could lift this plane," raising his arms above his head in a hoisting motion.

Despite such inestimable benefits, the deleterious health effects of khat are both abundant and unpalatable. Short-term withdrawal symptoms include depression, irritability, nightmares, constipation, and tremors, while long-term use of the drug can lead to ulcers, decreased liver function, tooth decay, and possibly some forms of mental illness. The physical ills of the drug are compounded by its social ones; the UN World Food Programme, for example, has reported that in some areas of Puntland the high costs associated with khat consumption are the main reason for not sending children to school (primary school fees are about eight dollars per month) as well as for high divorce rates.[6]

There are also some not-so-scientifically-documented effects. My Somali host, Abdirizak, claimed that khat causes sperm to leak into men's urine—eventually rendering them infertile—which he humorously cited as the principal reason that frustrated wives try at all costs to keep their husbands away from it. Like many folk-medicine theories, Abdi's may have had a basis in truth; there is some evidence that long-term khat abuse can lead to a diminished sex drive. In the short term, conversely, it can have quite the opposite effect.

"When some men chew khat, they need to have a woman immediately," Abdi once explained to me. "They can't control themselves." Indeed, those who prepped me for my own khat experience agreed that the drug would bring about one of two scenarios: I would either become relaxed and talkative, or a sex-crazy maniac bent on immediate satiation. But after all the buildup, I didn't feel much of anything. Four hours of chewing the bitter filth made me sweaty, jittery, sick to my stomach, and, finally, mildly contented. It did not strike me as an equitable trade-off, yet those who can afford it spend their days chewing khat leaves like a cow on her cud.

In the end, I chewed khat six or seven times during my visits to Puntland, out of perverse pragmatism. In spite of a lifetime of exposure to anti-drug public service ads, I continued chewing simply to fit in. More accurately, I discovered that khat was an incredible interviewing tool; it rendered my interviewees relaxed and talkative, with a compelling urge to express themselves. Interviews could go on for hours so long as the khat continued to flow.

* * *

There are few comprehensive academic studies of the Somali khat trade, and any attempt to obtain accurate information on the khat economy suffers from the general dearth of official statistics about Somalia. The latest government figures come from a 2003 report by the Puntland Ministry of Planning and Statistics, which devotes less than one of its sixty pages to the topic. Concluding with the vague assertion that "khat trade and consumption play an adverse role in the Somali economy in general and particularly in Puntland," the report nonetheless provides some concrete figures (see Table 1).[7]

Table 1: Estimated Imports of Khat to Puntland, 2003 (Kilograms)		
Type	Per month	Per year
Mirra, imported from Kenya	90,700	1,088,000
Hareeri, imported from Ethiopia	121,300	1,456,000
Total	212,000	2,544,000
		Source: Puntland Ministry of Planning and Statistics

These statistics are enough to construct a rudimentary sketch of the Puntland khat industry of nine years ago. Urban street prices for khat, according to my sources, have remained fairly steady at twenty dollars per kilogram over the last decade (in remote areas the price can be almost double), suggesting that total revenues in 2003 fell just short of $51 million. Using the UN Development Programme's 2006 Puntland population estimate of 1.3 million, the per capita consumption rate would be around 2.1 kilograms per person. However, khat consumers in Puntland are almost without exception men, and after narrowing the field to males aged fifteen and over,[8] annual per capita consumption climbs to 9.1 kilograms, worth about $180. Other sources support this estimate; for example, a 2001 study

by the UN's Water and Sanitation Programme found that poor consumers (the vast majority of Puntlanders) spent an average of $176
per year on the drug.

These numbers, however, are from the pre-piracy era. How
might they look in 2012? Attempting to gauge piracy's effect on khat
sales in Puntland, I spoke to three Garowe-based merchants. The
first was the aforementioned Fadumo, a bored-looking middle-aged
woman with stylish beige sunglasses pushed up on the headdress of
her fuchsia *guntiino* (a garment similar to a sari). My second conversation was with a pair of close friends in their late twenties, Maryan
and Faiza, who owned side-by-side stalls in the khat *suq*. (I later discovered that Maryan—probably the most stunning Somali woman I
had ever seen—was a member of Garaad's rumoured harem of wives,
a fact she admitted with an embarrassed giggle, asking how I had
learned of it.)[9]

Fadumo worked long hours, from ten in the morning until ten at
night. Her most profitable period was from one to three in the afternoon, when government employees got off work; four o'clock, the
time that construction workers finished their day, heralded another
mini rush hour. Her best days came at the end of the month, when
soldiers were paid, and the two or three times per year that Puntland's parliament was in session. "When there's an election, that's the
very best time," she said, because each candidate would arrive with a
large entourage in tow, filling Garowe's hotels to capacity.

When asked how piracy had affected her sales, Fadumo shot me
an incredulous look, as if the answer were self-evident. "Most pirates
spend money on three things: khat, alcohol, and women," was her
reply. "Also, very young people chew it now," she added.

Fadumo estimated that the booming khat *suq* provided a livelihood to over two hundred vendors. One reason for the abundance
of merchants is that launching a khat business requires no capital
outlay; distributors are happy to supply a new vendor on consignment. "Only one and a half years ago," Fadumo said, "khat suppliers
were coming and knocking at our doors, begging us to be sellers.

Now there are too many dealers . . . the market is flooded with them." Back then, there would be days when she would only earn 20,000 to 30,000 shillings ($0.60–$0.90) profit, and occasionally she would not have any customers at all. At the time I interviewed her in June 2009, her gross revenue for an average day had risen to about $550–$600, of which Fadumo kept $100–$110 of profit. There was so much competition, she told me, that in order to get a high-quality product she had to be proactive; on many days she would travel up to thirty kilometres outside of Garowe to intercept the earliest shipments before they reached the city.

Kenyan khat was far more popular with her customers, and Fadumo did not even bother to stock the Ethiopian variety. The same went for Maryan and Faiza. "People say *mirra* [Kenyan khat] gets you in a better mood," explained Faiza.

Piracy had also made a big difference to Maryan's and Faiza's balance sheets.

"The men have more money," Maryan said. "They buy larger amounts and they don't ask for loans."

"We've had a lot of problems with loans in the past," said Faiza. "They take the khat from you when they can't afford it, and they won't pay you back."

"The pirates pay in cash, nothing less," said Maryan, smiling broadly.

While men are the exclusive consumers of khat, those who sell it to them are almost exclusively women. According to Maryan, the collapse of the central state had forced Somali women to be more self-reliant. "The men are mainly unemployed," said Maryan, "and the women have been forced to earn money to pay the bills, school fees, and things like that. They have to work to survive. Khat is a very reliable source of income."

Perhaps one reason for its reliability is the fact that its price remains remarkably stable. But in a city where a cappuccino costs twenty-five cents, and where the majority of residents have no steady job, the twenty dollars required to maintain a steady high over the course of a day makes khat as expensive and luxurious a plant as medieval saffron. So prohibitive is the cost that I was continually baffled by the round-the-clock crowds chewing in the streets, against a backdrop of poverty and squalor; the steady influx of pirate dollars in recent years seemed the easiest explanation. Indeed, piracy has weighted so much of the daily economic life in Puntland towards the buying, bargaining, and bartering of khat that Puntlanders would perhaps do well to junk their near-worthless currency and adopt one based on the "khat standard."

On top of its numerous other negative effects, khat is a huge drain on Somalia's foreign exchange holdings, sending hundreds of millions of US dollars per year to Kenya and Ethiopia at the expense of domestic investment;[10] it was for this reason that former dictator Mohamed Siad Barre tried extensively (and hopelessly) to stamp out khat use in the 1980s. Piracy, which is one of Puntland's best foreign exchange earners, ultimately does little to improve economic opportunity on the ground, because pirate ransoms are continually recycled back into international markets via khat and Land Cruiser purchases.

* * *

Though ubiquitous amongst the local people, khat use is generally viewed by Somali expats as a sordid and disreputable activity, and many consider it a national shame. President Farole's virulent hatred of khat is well known, and he has been heard to vow that one day Somali men will feel shame at ever having chewed the plant.

Medically speaking, khat may be less physically harmful than many other legal drugs—such as alcohol and tobacco—but its social impact is another matter. Because of the many hours required to feel its full effects, chewing khat is a time-consuming activity, necessitating a large portion of the day. While a six-pack after a hard day or an occasional smoke break can fit into the restrictions of a nine-to-five schedule, a society-wide khat addiction seems unsustainable in a modern economy. So long as the majority of Puntlanders remain un- or underemployed, khat will remain a second-tier scourge. But if and when Puntland—and Somalia in general—rejoin the rest of the world, the increasing trend of khat consumption will present a serious public policy problem for the future government.

One need only look across the Gulf of Aden for a preview of Somalia's potential fate. In Yemen, 40 per cent of the country's precious groundwater is devoted to growing khat, Yemeni men routinely take their families on "khat picnics," and it is not unusual for government ministers to chew the plant continuously in their offices. Commentators often speak of the "oil curse" that stunts the political growth of many Middle Eastern and African nations; perhaps Puntland is lucky to have avoided the "water curse" that would have permitted widespread domestic cultivation of the crop.[11]

Jamal, my plane companion, described how he once saw a billy goat munching on a bundle of fallen khat leaves. When he had finished, the goat went trotting after the nearest female, attempting to mount her several times before giving up; the khat had evidently rendered him temporarily impotent. Jamal laughed: "It's the same with humans." If the problem is not addressed, Puntlanders might find that the khat epidemic poses a similarly vexing impediment to their nation-building goals.

* * *

For all of khat's sundry evils, it is the way to a pirate's heart. One June day during my second visit to Puntland, Boyah and some of his former gang agreed to spend the afternoon with me, for a small price: an all-you-can-chew khat buffet. As soon as the midday transport trucks had coming rolling into Garowe, Colonel Omar Abdullahi Farole—my host Mohamad's cousin—headed to the khat market with my eighty dollars in his pocket, enough to buy roughly four kilograms of the plant, which was to last us the day.

My translator on this trip, Omar, who was another of President

Farole's sons, and I picked up Boyah just outside his house, on a rundown street littered with old tires and scrap metal. I had not seen him since our meeting four months before, but he remembered me, acknowledging my presence with a brief nod and a half-smile before turning and climbing into the Land Cruiser's passenger seat. The Colonel, meanwhile, busied himself across town rounding up a few of Boyah's former colleagues into an old station wagon; with his arms overflowing with khat, it was not a difficult assignment.

Soon we were tearing along the main road out of Garowe, breaking off after ten minutes to join the dirt trail leading to the cooperative farm where I had first met Boyah. A short time later the station wagon pulled up and parked alongside the Land Cruiser; inside were Colonel Omar and two of Boyah's former running mates: Momman (a nickname) and a man I will call Ali Ghedi. The gathering soon assumed the atmosphere of a picnic, with eager hands offloading the day's supplies: *dirins* (woven mats), thermoses of sweet tea, bottles of water, packs of cigarettes, and the half-dozen black plastic shopping bags containing the khat. We unfurled the *dirins* in the shade of a broad-limbed acacia tree and settled down, tossing our sandals into the dirt. A short distance away, a dishevelled young farmhand sat in the shade of a wooden shack, absorbedly chewing a few stems of khat that one of the pirates had handed him.

As soon as we had settled down on our *dirins*, I reached into my bag and pulled out the thank-you gift I had brought for Boyah, in appreciation of his willingness to be open with me: an Alex Rios Toronto Blue Jays T-shirt. He broke into a broad grin, immediately removing his own shirt and putting it on. "Is it official?" he asked, and I answered that it was. "How much did you pay for it?"

The Colonel laid his mat a dozen paces distant and flopped down on it, the crook of his elbow covering his eyes. He had been khat sober for thirty-two days, part of an all-around cleansing policy that granted few exemptions: "Only in wartime, when things get a little stressful," he explained. Colonel Omar, I had learned weeks ago, was not really a colonel. A battle-hardened militiaman, the Colonel had fought in the south alongside former Puntland president Abdullahi Yusuf against the Islamist militant group Al-Shabaab, one of three conflicts he claimed to have participated in; after each, he said, he had promoted himself by one rank. "I'm going to Ethiopia soon to receive training," he had told me. "When I get back, I'll be a general."

The sun was mild and a light breeze was blowing, a pleasant change from the gale-force winds constantly sweeping Garowe. Taking periodic breaks from the khat, Boyah opened a small plastic bag and removed a pinch or so of chewing tobacco, depositing it gingerly into his mouth. The conversation turned to sundry topics: women, Omega-3 fatty acids, naming customs. The pirates collectively warned me that the khat would make me sexually aroused, to the point that my urge for a woman would be unbearable; I informed them that I had chewed it before, experiencing no such effect. "The white people we see in porn movies are always so horny," said Momman. "So how is it that you're not?"

Mobile phones chimed like persistent alarm clocks every few minutes, each member of the circle splitting his conversational energies between his phone and the people around him in almost equal measure. One particularly harsh voice blaring from Momman's phone, allegedly belonging to a member of Al-Shabaab, piqued my attention. My interpreter Omar summarized the exchange: the caller expressed displeasure that Momman's pirate earnings, in his opinion, had gone not to support the Somali people but to fund President Farole's political campaign, and he warned Momman that he might have to forfeit his life to atone for these sins. Momman remained curiously calm throughout the call; when I expressed my concern, he waved it off with one hand and told me that these threats happened daily as a matter of course. Shabaab apparently conducted its terror campaigns not only through assassinations and suicide bombings, but over the airwaves of Somali telecom networks.

Omar selected one of the half-dozen Kalashnikovs lying scattered around us—which he had recently purchased for the high-end price of $600—and declared that it must be tested. I jumped to my feet and eagerly volunteered for the assignment. Omar and I moved past the hedge marking the boundary of the farm to the banks of the trickling Nugaal River, which was struggling with its last rebellious spurts against the encroaching dry season.

Countless hours of news footage of obscure post-Cold War insurgencies had not prepared me for the raw, ear-shattering power of the AK-47. The two shots I fired into the river's embankment seemed to make the whole earth boom and shake, until I realized that it was my own body being contorted by the force of the recoil. By comparison, the faint bursts of dust marking where the bullets hit were sadly anti-climactic. I returned to the gathering with a stupid grin stretching across my face, and was greeted by an array of patronizing smiles from the circle of pirates—the look of hardened veterans at the overzealous enthusiasm of an amateur.

I didn't bother with any interview questions that day, but chatted amiably and did my best to blend in with the boys. My goal was achieved when, late in the afternoon, the pirates began discussing something between themselves in hushed voices. They appeared to reach a consensus, at which point Momman turned to me: "We've decided that you're a cool guy," he said.

It had been a day well spent.

* * *

Two days later, we returned to the same spot, arms weighted down with even bulkier bags of khat—and thus with a commensurately larger pirate gathering in tow. Boyah, when we picked him up on the side of the road, let us know that he had had a rough night. "I was terribly sick with a kidney problem," he said. "I thought I was going to die, so I said goodbye to my kids. But I'm feeling much better today." He hopped into the 4x4 and waited patiently for us to get under way.

Two other cars joined us, bringing the total gathering of pirates to seven: Boyah, Momman, Ali Ghedi, Mohammad Duale (I have changed his name), Ahmed Jadob, and two others to whom I was not properly introduced. Much like last time, we rolled out the *dirins* and flopped down, propped up on our elbows. Pulling two bundles of the wilting leaves out of the bag, Boyah offered me my pick. I hesitated for a moment before I remembered an earlier crash course in khat quality given to me by the Colonel. Quickly scanning the bundle, I chose the bunch with the greatest abundance of red-tinged stems. Boyah smiled, laughed, and slapped my leg playfully, uttering some words of praise. He was still wearing the Blue Jays shirt, evidenced by the powder-blue collar poking out from under his cotton overshirt.

The reason these men were so willing to talk to me went beyond the complimentary khat. When I had last seen him, four months ago, Boyah had been on a personal quest to atone for his past misdeeds. Now, it seemed, his feelings of remorse had spread to his former colleagues: each of the men around me claimed to have renounced piracy, never to return to his former trade—and they wanted people to know it. "It wasn't good, either for us or our country," explained Boyah. "It's cursed money—it only made our lives worse. So we quit. We don't want to get a bad name in foreign countries."

When I suggested that the recent proliferation of warships off the Somali coast had provided an equally compelling reason to turn in one's rocket-propelled grenades and grappling ladder, I was met with a round of scornful laughter. "Don't think that we're scared," said Boyah. "Piracy is just not good for us. We're quitting so that Somalia can get its nice name back. Seven months ago . . . French and US forces were killing us, and we didn't stop then."

As had been the case two days ago, my companions fell into relaxed conversation, hardly conscious of my presence. For people who had never set foot outside Somalia and had access to no more than a few local TV stations, Boyah and his entourage were surprisingly worldly: Momman and Ali Ghedi engaged in an animated debate about whether France or Brazil boasted the most beautiful women.

There was a lull in the conversation, and Ali, having just learned that I had fired a Kalashnikov for the first time two days ago, turned and brazenly challenged me to a shooting contest.

"*Laag?*" For money? I asked, showing off one of the few Somali words I knew.

"Yes, for money," he replied, with a crooked grin. I gestured to the backgammon board I had brought along with me, and asked him if he would match my wager on the gun with his own wager on the dice. He meekly demurred.

* * *

Since giving up the piracy trade, Boyah and his men had put their time to good use. Garaad, whose dealings with SomCan had begun some months earlier, had spread his career ambitions to his former colleagues—or so my sources said; the rumours were that Boyah's gang had also recently entered a partnership with the SomCan Coast Guard. But I soon discovered that the rumours were out of date. "We used to work with them, but that's all over," said Boyah. "What they wanted and what we needed were totally different." What Boyah's men had needed, apparently, was a fresh start.

"We want to start our *own* coast guard," he said. "In fact, we've already started." Their efforts to date, however, had not extended much beyond signing up the men presently lounging around me. "We're hoping the Puntland government will give us the job," said Boyah. "Once they do, we'll get the ships and weapons we need from them." Until then, it seemed, Boyah's coast guard would remain landlocked. His confidence, nonetheless, was unshaken.

"We know how to fight with pirates," he said. "You can't teach us anything about hijacking ships." But immediately his bellicose tone softened: "Of course, we would never kill anyone, even the pirates. There are other ways—peaceful ways—we can get them to release the ships. Before you shoot someone, you can talk to him. If we were in charge, no one would ever have to pay any ransoms, nor would anyone ever die on those ships. We would work it out some way." Despite my pressing, Boyah and his colleagues would not be more specific about what their method would entail.

In defiance of Boyah's optimism were the two ships currently being held hostage at Eyl, their hijackers unreceptive to his efforts at moral suasion. For these men, Boyah had a simple explanation. "They still have the old system in their heads, and they don't want to let it go. Plus, they've already spent so much money while waiting for the ransom. If they leave it now without being paid, there are thousands of people they owe money to who will kill them. Maybe when they get off they'll change their minds, and not return to piracy."

For all his talk of persuasion, Boyah believed that a military solution would be just as effective. "If a warship attacked them, they would run, just like we would have," said Boyah. "These people are not Al-Qaeda; they just want money. They don't kill people."

On land, Boyah claimed that his group was already making a difference. Under the guidance of preeminent Muslim scholar (and Puntland's unofficial grand mufti) Sheikh Abdulkhadar Nur Farah, Boyah's gang of reformed pirates had taken on a role similar to the ex-convicts who speak to high school student assemblies; along with Sheikh Farah, Boyah and his men would drag groups of misguided youth to mosque, where they would make them swear on the Koran to live piracy-free for the rest of their days. According to Boyah, his group had helped reform seven hundred pirates and would-be pirates from around Puntland (though the BBC, which had run the story three weeks earlier, reported the number of rehabilitated pirates at around two hundred).[12] Altruism was probably not Boyah's sole motive, however; in exchange for their efforts, the Puntland government had granted Boyah and his associates full legal amnesty for their past crimes.

Their services as coast guards, on the other hand, were not being so eagerly sought. President Farole was on his own quest to rehabilitate Puntland's damaged international reputation, and commissioning an ex-pirate brigade, composed of his own clan members, as his coast guard would not serve the image he was seeking. Though their redemption movement had been used as PR fodder by the Puntland government—as evidence of measures the new administration was taking to combat piracy—Farole had no plans to unleash Boyah and company once more onto the sea.

*　*　*

Up to this point, Boyah had been the only member of the gathering to answer my questions, while the others nodded along complacently as he talked. "Boyah speaks for all of us," Momman responded, when I commented on this fact. In an attempt to engage with someone other than Boyah, I directed my questions to Ahmed, who was atypically dressed in a glaringly bright yellow soccer jersey. Beyond his attire, Ahmed also stuck out in another way: he was from the Hawiye clan, whereas all the others assembled were Darod. Originally from the southern city of Baidoa, he had emigrated to Eyl in 2002 and become a successful fisherman. Despite the historical animosity between the Hawiye and the Darod—which came to a head with the brutal clan pogroms of the early 1990s—history seemed to have been forgotten amongst this group of friends. "We pirates have no clans," said Boyah. "We fight together as Somalis."

At my urging, Ahmed began to relate his story. "I was happy with my life," he said. "One day, we were fishing some distance away from shore when we were attacked by some big fishing ships, who stole all our fish." This event was repeated, he said, at least ten times. "They had big guns, and we would be forced to jump overboard. Sometimes, they would destroy our boats and we would have to swim all the way back to shore." According to Ahmed, the culprits were most often Thai or Korean fishing vessels. In what was by now a common story, Ahmed had banded together with similarly aggrieved fishermen along the length of the Puntland coast and beyond to fight illegal fishing.

Groups like these resembled troops of revolutionaries more than criminal gangs, yet Western media sources invariably associated

Somali pirates with a glamorous lifestyle akin to that of gangster rap stars, replete with lavish parties, mansions, luxury cars, drugs, alcohol, and beautiful women. But other than their habitual khat binges, little evidence of this stereotype was to be seen in the sedate, stoic (and now resurgently pious) figures of Boyah and his men. Each of them, as far as I had been able to discover, had but one wife. So what was to be said for the stories of "pirate wenches"?

"There are some women like that . . . the drug addicts, the bad ones," said Boyah. "The ones interested in money." These pirate women, according to Boyah, were not local, but came from outside Puntland. Indeed, a roadhouse on the outskirts of Garowe—one that I had passed many times—had reportedly served in the past as a major transit hub for transporting women to Puntland's coastal areas. But in Boyah's estimation, the women were more than able to find their own way. "They follow the money," he said.

Mohammad turned to Boyah with a quizzical look. "I haven't even seen the women you're talking about," he said.

The same incredulity greeted my question about pirates and alcohol consumption, and generated a round of unmistakably hostile murmurs and head shakes.

"We're Muslims, so we don't do that," came the answer.

"Some of them do—the young guys." Boyah clarified. "They try it because it's something new that they haven't experienced before."

Such may have been the case on board a Russian-crewed hostage vessel, on which the pirates reportedly drank the ship's entire store of vodka, stunning even the Russians with their debauchery. When I brought up this rumour, I again witnessed a round of shaking heads.

"No, no. They drank a little bit, but not to that extent," said Boyah. "They had a job to do. If they had gotten drunk, do you think they would have done it? Anyone who gets drunk, they kick off the ship."

Colonel Omar, lying on his back apart from the main circle, suddenly chimed in with his own version of events. "There *was* one boat with a lot of alcohol on board," he said. "So the pirates threw it all into the sea, and when the crew asked for it, they told them that they had drunk it all." Mohammad nodded his assent to the Colonel's account.

We continued chewing our khat as the sky grew dark, faces fading into the twilight until only the glowing points of cigarettes marked their locations. Abruptly, the Colonel roused himself from his nearby reverie and declared that the time had come to leave—the heightened risk of kidnapping made my presence a security liability at nighttime, even at a location as remote and isolated as this farm.

As we rolled up the *dirins* and collected our garbage—to be dumped by the side of the main road—Boyah admonished me to tell the story of him and his men exactly as they had given it to me. "Something good has to come back to us from all of this," he said.

By the time we had pulled back onto the road it was fully dark. The white outline of the pirates' Mark II station wagon was visible ahead of us, growing closer as Omar gunned our Land Cruiser towards it. The needle on the speedometer pushed past 140 kilometres per hour before we overtook the Mark II, passing it with a few fist-widths to spare. If this was the typical driving style on this unlit, steeply embanked roadway, the stripped chassis and blackened wrecks I routinely saw by the side of the road needed no explanation. We left the Mark II behind as we barrelled towards the lights of Garowe.

7

The Land of Punt

IT WAS JUNE, AND GAROWE WAS IN THE MIDST OF THE HAGAA, the second of Puntland's two dry seasons. It had been a month since rain last fell, and it would be three months before the next rain would come. The bridge over the Nugaal River spanned a vast, rocky emptiness; further down its course, the last vestiges of the wet season had dried to isolated, listless pools. In the evenings, the haunting refrains of *Allahu akbar* drifted from the muezzins over a ruddy landscape strewn with rusted cans, broken glass, and camel tracks. Garbage carpeted the streets; at an improvised dump at the outskirts of town, thousands of plastic bags caught in thorny shrubs formed a vast artificial garden.

Since the collapse of the central state, the city has sprawled outwards, unchecked; over the last two decades Garowe's population has multiplied eightfold, swelled by the influx of Darod clanspeople fleeing the violence in the south. Virtually ignored under the dictatorship of Mohamed Siad Barre, the returning migrants inherited no infrastructure, financial base, or skilled bureaucracy, and were forced to build a functioning polity out of an empty desert.

With a paltry $20 million annual budget that often fails to include items as basic as civil service salaries, it comes as no surprise that Puntland officials at all levels have been accused of systematically accepting bribes and payouts from pirate gangs in exchange for turning a blind eye. My own impression, however, was that there were few local officials actually worth bribing. State power was extremely decentralized and diffuse, and the military forces were highly immobile and mostly confined to garrisons in the large cities. In the smaller towns the government had virtually no presence, and certainly no armed force capable of matching firepower with even the smallest of pirate gangs.

Yet, in spite of the logistical difficulties it faces—not to mention the suspicions about its own complicity—the Puntland government appears bent on proving to the world that it alone is capable of neutralizing the pirates on land.

* * *

Officially, the government of Puntland has advocated a strict policy of non-negotiation with pirates since the very beginning of the crisis. Former president Mohamud Muse Hersi, though himself accused of receiving ransom kickbacks, blamed the piracy problem on the willingness of international shippers to accede to the hijackers' demands. "Can you reward a thief who mugged you?" said Hersi in an interview. "This money makes them stronger and encourages them to carry out more operations. We should never give in to their blackmailing." [1]

Hersi's words were not empty. Where his government was given permission to act, it did not hesitate to confront the pirates head-on. In April 2008, for example, one hundred Puntland soldiers in several armoured boats stormed the UAE cargo ship *Al Khaleej* near Bossaso, capturing seven pirates, who were eventually sentenced to life in prison. Two soldiers and three hijackers sustained injuries, but the hostages were unharmed. A similar incident occurred in October of the same year, when (as described in Chapter 4) the Panamanian-flagged MV *Wail* was freed by the Puntland Coast Guard. In both cases, the ships had been contracted by local businessmen and were carrying consignments destined for Puntland.

Judging from the Puntland government's press statements, it is more than willing to send its security forces to storm every ship being held in its waters. The decision to employ force, however, lies with the vessels' owners, most of whom have no interest in authorizing a potential bloodbath on the decks of their ships.

Abdirahman Farole, who took over from Hersi as president in January 2009, was even more outwardly committed to cracking down on piracy, describing the practice as a black mark on Puntland's international reputation. Three months after his election, Farole launched a grassroots counter-piracy program spearheaded by Sheikh Abdulkhadar Nur Farah. In what was described as an "educational and spiritual campaign" to discourage new recruits, the government offered total amnesty to any former pirate agreeing to give up the trade.[2]

In the mosques, Muslim clerics decried the litany of social ills that piracy had supposedly introduced to the local community: alcohol, khat, sexually transmitted diseases, adultery, and fornication. To kick off the campaign, Puntland security forces conducted a highly publicized raid on two houses in Garowe, confiscating four assault rifles, 327 bottles of Ethiopian gin, five mobile phones, and approximately $900 in cash.[3] Spectators cheered as soldiers hauled away suspected pirates.

Farole's religious campaign has not been an isolated media exercise. Since coming to power, he has tried his best to promote his administration as a fresh break from the one previous, which was widely perceived by international observers as weak and ineffectual. The media wing of the Puntland government has issued a constant stream of press releases detailing raids, arrests, and imprisonments of active pirates—part of a sustained publicity campaign to market the administration abroad as a reliable ally in the war on piracy.

At home, Farole has relied on a network of local police commissioners and office holders to carry out his campaigns. One of these instrumental figures was Garowe's long-serving mayor, Abdulkhadar Osman Fod'Adde.

* * *

Garowe's mayoral office was situated in a rundown complex at the centre of town. A bare flagpole stood by the entrance to a crumbling courtyard; on the steps of the building, a small congregation of clan elders lounged in their *ma'awises,* idly discussing the matters of the day. Inside, the scene was markedly different: Abdulkhadar Fod'Adde sat behind a heavy cherry desk in a tidy and orderly office, dressed in a trim suit and tie. The two Omars had accompanied me, and I took a seat between them across the desk, the Colonel on my right, Kalashnikov slung over a shoulder, and Omar Farole to my left, serving as my interpreter.

"I worked for the previous government for two and a half years," Fod'Adde began. "It was the worst job I've ever had. That was a really bad government to work with; this one is much better. Security was really bad, especially last December," he continued. "There were a lot of pirates, and we couldn't do anything about it . . . we weren't given enough money. Under this government, there are fewer pirates, we have more money, and security is a lot better. We can see things getting better and better every day, and that encourages us to work hard at our jobs."

As Fod'Adde proceeded to draw out his panegyric over the course of several minutes, I was once more made conscious of being under the wing of the Farole family. With the Omars seated on either side of me, it was apparent that much of Fod'Adde's monologue was being tailored for the ears of the president's son and cousin.

Sycophancy aside, the security situation had improved since the days of the previous administration. President Hersi had discontinued the pay of the security forces and civil service in early 2008, a decision that unquestionably contributed to the rise of piracy towards the end of the year. When Farole took power in January 2009, he immediately reinstated civil payrolls and began to reorganize the Darawish, Puntland's security forces. Even in the three-month interval between my first and second visits to the region, the improvements to security had been remarkable: soldiers positioned at regular checkpoints throughout the city checked every passing vehicle, tinted windows had been prohibited, and there had been a successful campaign to get guns off the streets. At night, security patrols swept through the city and the surrounding desert, combing them for pirates and weapons smugglers.

The change, based on the stories I had heard, had been monumental. Garowe in late 2008 had been, by all accounts, practically run by pirates, with opulent weddings attended by processions of 4x4s and khat-fuelled festivities a common sight. It was an assessment that Fod'Adde corroborated.

"Once they got the ransom money the pirates would come to Garowe," he said. "Then they'd get drunk, start gunfights in the street, things like that. Things very much against our culture."

On what did they spend their money? I asked.

"Ladies," Fod'Adde instantly replied. "They ruin families by stealing women away from their husbands. The women can smell the money . . . A lot of the women come from Somaliland, Djibouti, and other places in Somalia, so they bring a lot of diseases."

The view that outside women were somehow tainted—which seemed to be based solely on raw clan prejudice—was shared by many of Garowe's leading citizens; at the beginning of Farole's anti-piracy campaign, one cleric strongly warned his Friday congregation against the spread of HIV/AIDS in the community, as "prostitutes from everywhere" had been drawn to Puntland by the pirates' money.[4]

Piracy, nonetheless, represented a massive injection of foreign exchange into the Puntland economy, and it was hard to imagine that there had been no positive trickle-down effects. Fod'Adde shook his head vigorously. "That money is *haram* [religiously forbidden]," he said. "As Muslims, we believe that money earned in that manner can never do any good . . . not for the economy or anything else. The moment they get it, they waste it on women, drugs, khat . . . *haram* money never stays in one's pocket for long."

Nor could the new houses springing up atop the carcass of the

former airport, providing a boost to Garowe's already booming construction industry, convince him that pirate dollars would bring any
benefits. "The pirates had all this money, but no experience with
business," he said. "So they pay the workers five hundred dollars
per day, when normally they might be paid fifty. And so the workers themselves start chewing khat all the time, and they get used to
the high pay and now are no longer happy to take regular jobs. You
know, the more money you get paid, the lazier you get."

In any case, said Fod'Adde, the reports of pirate construction
sprees had been grossly overstated. "That's not the way that most of
them spend their money," he said. "I'd say that only one in a hundred
actually builds a house. As for the houses that they do build, they
can't rent them and no one buys them, because they're *haram*. So the
pirates are stuck with them."

At this point, my interpreter Omar could not resist interrupt-
ing with his own anecdote. "Even the cars they buy are *haram*," he
said. "If we see one driving by, my dad says, 'Don't buy that one. It's
a *haram* car . . . a pirate car.'"

As proof of the curse of pirate cash, Fod'Adde brought up the
case of Kadiye, a famed pirate leader who had recently returned
from a Kenyan hospital after reportedly breaking both legs when he
crashed his 4x4. Kadiye's house, a sprawling structure by the side
of the road at the northern outskirts of Garowe, suggested an evis-
cerated corpse, the whitewash of its outer walls terminating around
gaping holes of exposed brick. "Look at Kadiye. He earned about
three million dollars, but he didn't have any plan," Fod'Adde said.
"He spent seventy thousand dollars on that house, but couldn't fin-
ish it. He blew all his money on girls, and now he doesn't have one
cent left."

As I prepared to leave, Fod'Adde seamlessly resumed his earlier extolling of the present government's efforts to combat piracy:
"Some of the pirates have been killed, some have no money left, and
some have gone overseas. But we're always looking around for them,
and if we catch any we send them to the prison in Bossaso.

"We don't even see them anymore. We ask ourselves, were they ghosts or human beings?" he said, laughing.

*   *   *

Bossaso prison lies a kilometre down a bumpy path jutting off the main road at the southern outskirts of the city. The square fortress-like structure with outer walls of pale yellow stands alone in an empty expanse, with nothing in the vicinity but stony rubble and the distant outline of the Karkaar Mountains. At opposing corners of the building stand two monolithic guard towers, whose sentries shout out demands for identification from the occupants of any vehicle passing within range of their assault rifles. Like runway markers, lines of carefully placed stones trace out the correct approach vector to the prison's imposing blue gateway.

Built with UN Development Programme money, this is one of two prisons serving a population of 1.3 million; the other, 250 kilometres south in the town of Qardho, is not yet operational. (There are also two rundown jails, located in Garowe and Galkayo.) With an incarcerated population of about one person per 5,000 (in the United States, the figure is one in 120), the fact that Puntland is not overrun by criminal gangs might seem inexplicable. The simple answer is that clan law (*heer*), not the rule of law, rules in Puntland. The state-administered justice system is, in a way, a last recourse in the event that clan mechanisms of dispute resolution fail.[5] Almost half the inmates of Bossaso prison are pirates, a consequence of the Puntland government's desire to demonstrate to the international community that it is serious about cracking down on piracy. It is unclear, however, under which law the men were charged; Puntland is still technically operating under the decades-old criminal code of the defunct Somali Republic, which lacks specific provisions for criminalizing piracy. Though Puntland's Islamic clerics have interpreted vague proscriptions in sharia law against the setting up of trade-disrupting "roadblocks" as applying to sea piracy, such an approach is hardly a substitute for a modern juridical process.

When I visited, Bossaso prison, meant for a capacity of 150, was jammed to the point of putrefaction with 275 ragged men. They were crammed into a half-dozen cells lining a central court-yard that doubled as an exercise yard. Beyond the chain-link fence surrounding the enclosure, the smell of urine saturated the July air. On the far side of the yard was the prison's approximation of a mental health ward, an orange tarp spread over a few barrels, underneath which a solitary man was shackled to the ground by his ankle. The man introduced himself as Dr. Osman, a "human rights victim" who had once lived in Virginia. A few moments later, a prison administrator introduced Dr. Osman as "a madman" who had been jailed for his own good after falsely claiming to be an Al-Shabaab agent.

At mealtimes, guards spooned helpings of gruel into the prison-ers' cupped shirts, or, if they lacked an intact garment, directly into their hands. On alternating days, half the prison population was let out into the yard to exercise. The atmosphere I observed was remi-niscent of a school playground: some inmates congregated in cor-ners, chatting and drinking milky tea out of plastic water bottles, while others kicked soccer balls across the crumbling concrete or launched basketballs at half-detached hoops. Their less fortunate colleagues pressed up against their cell bars, looking on begrudg-ingly. On the walls above the courtyard guards perched like eagles, rifles laid flat across their squatting legs.

My first of two visits to the prison had taken place on a very special day: a presidential visit by Abdirahman Farole. I had been accompanying the president for over a week as he travelled north from Garowe to Bossaso on his first domestic tour since his election. In each town and hamlet along the way, cheering throngs had wel-comed him with joyous ululations, waving fronds and banging furi-ously on empty oil canisters. As his gold bulletproofed Land Cruiser pulled through the outer gate, he was greeted with even greater jubilation by the prison population, and for good cause: in celebration of his inauguration, about sixty minor offenders were to receive presidential pardons—a necessary measure to free up much-needed space in the overcrowded prison for more serious criminals.

The president did not disappoint; after delivering a speech to an assembly of prisoners, his soldiers, arms overflowing with stacks of bills, doled out release grants to the pardoned men, each of whom received one million shillings (this grant, worth about thirty dollars, was enough to buy about a day and a half's worth of khat in the local *suq*).

As the president's inspection tour moved towards the prison's living quarters, three pirate inmates were brought out to me in the outer courtyard, where we sat down on a set of flimsy plastic lawn chairs. Two wore striped tracksuits, the other, slacks and a blue dress shirt; all three appeared to be in a state of robust health that defied the conditions in which they lived. I soon learned that one of the men, Jamal, was Boyah's younger brother. Like his sibling, Jamal seemed to have a natural inclination towards leadership; seating himself directly across from me, he proceeded to field the majority of my questions. His two colleagues sat calmly smoking on either side of him, occasionally blurting out angry responses. Within a few minutes, a crowd of soldiers and prison officials had gathered around us, and the bodies pressing against my back forced me to hunch over my notebook.

"What we were doing wasn't illegal," Jamal began. "We were chasing after illegal fishing ships. We were defending our seas." Like Boyah, the three claimed to have been lobster divers in Eyl. They had habitually sold their catch to Somali middlemen in Bossaso, they said, who had paid them up to twenty-five dollars per kilogram. One month before, the trio had been caught by the French navy in an act of piracy, and were later handed over to the Puntland authorities.

"We were all sentenced to life in prison without even being given a lawyer," said Jamal. "We want a retrial."

The length of their sentences seemed unbelievable, and I asked my interpreter to confirm that I had understood correctly. It seemed a gross injustice for Jamal to languish in prison while Boyah—who had publicly admitted to hijacking dozens of ships—was free to chew khat with Puntland soldiers.

Shifting tacks, I asked Jamal about the former Puntland Coast Guard's involvement with illegal fishing, but he ignored the question and continued as if he were reading from a press release: "As fishermen, we were victims of every kind of ship crossing this planet: Western, Asian, whatever."

I repeated the question, but the result was the same.

"They dump toxins in our waters, and no one cares," he said. "Hopefully, the new government has some new ideas, and we can talk to them about what's going on and the problems we have." It was a strange attitude for men whose life sentences meant that their future problems would presumably be contained within these four walls.

Neither Jamal nor his colleagues would shed any light on the circumstances of their capture, not even the type of ship they had been pursuing when they were caught. But Jamal's next statement suggested that the gang had not been as focused on illegal fishing as he had initially indicated. "Fishing boats are hard to capture, they have more sophisticated defences," he said. "But the cargo ships are from the same countries and they are the same people. Our enemies are the ones doing the illegal fishing, but we'll take anything we can get. We don't discriminate."

Jamal's attack group had consisted of nine men, a typical pirate hunting party. The gang had employed two skiffs: one, a transport, carried the fuel, food, and water, while the other, speedier boat carried their rifles and rocket-propelled grenade launcher. When a suitable target was sighted, the entire team would transfer to the attack shuttle for the chase.

As I began my next question, the president and his entourage emerged from the inner compound and started to make their way slowly towards the outer gate. Without a word to me, the three rose in unison and rushed to intercept him. The president's security stood idly by as they inserted themselves in his path, performing slight bows as they lined up before him; he responded by shaking each of their hands warmly, almost as if they were prospective supporters on the campaign trail. I could understand nothing of their verbal exchange, but I knew that any hope for a pardon they may have held was dashed when the president turned and continued towards his waiting Land Cruiser.

In all likelihood, they would not have to wait too much longer for an early parole. If their relatives and friends did not manage to get them released through clan or political influence, their places in the prison would sooner or later be claimed by a future wave of offenders, part of the ongoing game of musical cells in the Puntland justice system. It was a problem that the Puntland government itself was aware of. "Every time a suspect is apprehended for a crime, there is a whole clan behind him, paying bribes, lying to officials," President Farole announced in a November 2010 public address. "The question is: who should be arrested then if the clans keep interfering on behalf of criminal suspects. Should only the people from outside [of Puntland] be arrested?"[6]

Even if the government were to release all non-pirate inmates, Puntland simply lacks the capacity to handle a steady stream of detainees from the international naval forces. With no domestic victims, piracy is clearly not a matter suited to inter-clan mediation, and, short of international seafarers' unions agreeing to abide by Somali customary law, Puntland will remain unable to carry its share of the burden without international assistance.

* * *

In the case of Boyah and company, of course, the response of the Puntland justice system had been to grant them total amnesty for their past crimes.

One afternoon, as I was chewing khat with Joaar, the director general of the Puntland Ministry of Fisheries (and Boyah's former employer in the lobster business), the subject of Boyah and Garaad's coast guard project came up. "Boyah and Garaad should be behind bars," Joaar declared, around a pulpy mouthful. "The idea of them serving as our coast guard is an insult." Boyah, said Joaar, had tried to meet with him on multiple occasions, but Joaar had refused because he feared that the two might be photographed together.

"Boyah called me just the other day to ask me why I was fighting against him," he said. "I told him: 'I want to eliminate you and all others like you' . . . The young guys can be rehabilitated, but the big criminals—the ones we call in Italian the *grande pesce* [big fish]— should be locked up."

Yet Boyah, Garaad, and other well-known pirate leaders still walked free. I once asked a Puntland government insider why Bossaso prison was overflowing with rank-and-file pirates, while the leaders remain on the outside. "The Puntland government can't arrest people based on rumours," he answered. "Also, because of clan loyalty, no witnesses would come forward. It's like having to make a case against a mafia boss." This explanation was somewhat disingenuous; mafia bosses generally do not publicly admit to their crimes, as Boyah had on multiple occasions.

Some, predictably, have imputed more insidious motives to the Farole government's unwillingness to prosecute past (and present) pirate kingpins, namely that the president himself has been receiving handouts from the very leaders he ostensibly condemns. Since his election, the accusations against Farole have ranged from complicity to profiteering, and even to direct involvement in piracy. My own affiliation with the president's son, Mohamad Farole, has been cited as evidence in the mounting case against him; Mohamad's presence at my meetings with pirates had been referenced in multiple online articles aimed at incriminating him, and, by extension, his father.

Some of the strongest indictments have come from the UN Monitoring Group on Somalia, in language surprisingly impolitic for a United Nations body. Warning that the new administration was "nudging Puntland in the direction of becoming a criminal state," the group's March 2010 report cited evidence from unnamed first-hand sources that "senior Puntland officials, including President Farole and members of his Cabinet, notably the Minister of the Interior, General Abdullahi Ahmed Jama 'Ilkajir' . . . and the Minister for Internal Security, General Abdillahi Sa'iid Samatar, have received proceeds from piracy and/or kidnapping."[7]

Hoping to shed some light on these claims, I spoke with Matt Bryden, the monitoring group's Nairobi-based coordinator. Though Bryden refused to reveal the group's sources, he was adamant that there was little reason to doubt their credibility. "We had a wealth of evidence, both direct and indirect, from eyewitnesses to direct monetary transactions, to testimony from captured pirates themselves," he said. "We saw signed statements from convicted pirates who did not appear to have been coerced and who stood by these statements when we interviewed them. We had sources who were in the room when cash was delivered, and sources party to telephone calls where cash payments were being discussed."

During a videotaped interview with local news agency Garowe Online in late 2008, Boyah had claimed that 30 per cent of all ransom money went into the pockets of Puntland officials—a statistic he had denied to me multiple times since (possibly out of concern for embarrassing his newly powerful co-clansman, President Farole). It was a notion that Bryden endorsed. "Did [Boyah] pay 30 per cent to local leaders in Eyl? I would think not," he said. "It is reasonable to assume that what Boyah was referring to was the payments he made to senior officials."

In the West, a public official receiving money under such circumstances would be labelled corrupt. But in the Somali context, the label is not entirely appropriate. In Somalia, clan and politics are incestuously intertwined, and political life is based on loyalty to one's clan, not the state apparatus. When, as is generally the case, one sub-clan—in essence an extended family—dominates the machinery of government, money changing hands between its members is considered no more illicit than an aunt looking after the children when their parents are away. "From the outside, it's impossible to determine whether Boyah giving money to Farole would be an attempt to sweeten the administration, or simply a contribution to a not-so-distant kinsman," explained Bryden.

On a personal level, these allegations came as a shock; it was difficult for me to accept that a man with whom I had shared a table on multiple occasions, a soft-spoken academic who seemed to have a sincere distaste for piracy, and whom I genuinely admired, could be guilty of such hypocrisy. The behaviour also seemed inconsistent with his political past; while serving as planning minister during the previous administration of Mohamud Hersi, Farole had resigned his post in protest over a shady oil deal that the president had entered into with the Australian firm Range Resources—a contract that would have offered Farole as lucrative a kleptocratic opportunity as pirate handouts.[8]

Despite Bryden's claimed plethora of unnamed sources, there has only been one publicly documented case of a Puntland official, Omar Shafdero, being directly involved in piracy. Shafdero, an employee at the Ministry of Finance and a relative of former president Hersi, was arrested in February 2008 and accused of links to the gang responsible for hijacking the Russian tugboat *Svitzer Korsakov*.[9] Shafdero spent a short time in custody before being mysteriously released, after which he fled into exile in Somaliland.

But pirate cash, argued Bryden, had been particularly instrumental in funding political candidacies in the run-up to the 2009 presidential election. According to the UN Monitoring Group report, a prominent pirate leader, Fu'ad Warsame Hanaano, "had contributed over $200,000" to the election campaign of Farole's foremost opponent (and now interior minister), General Abdullahi Ilkajir—a member of Hanaano's sub-clan, the Warsangali. Farole, the report contends, "benefitted from much larger contributions to his political war chest."[10] During the pre-election period, Bryden claimed, "There was a lot of excitement, a lot of money was changing hands and people didn't worry too much about where it came from. Now, because of international scrutiny, the movement of money is quieter . . . people are much more cautious. But according to captive pirates, the payments to the administration are ongoing."

The accusations surrounding President Farole have been fuelled, in part, by the fact that he is a native of Eyl and belongs to the Muse Isse, the same sub-clan as Boyah, Garaad, and many other Puntland-based pirates. This affiliation with Eyl, ironically, has also placed Farole in a much better position to tackle piracy than his predecessor, General Hersi, whose bumbling efforts to fight piracy were once related to me by a Puntland journalist colleague.

In early 2008, as Hersi—who belongs to the Osman Mahamoud sub-clan—continued to lose local support and credibility, Eyl was steadily establishing itself as Somalia's forefront pirate base. Knowing that to enter Eyl with his Osman Mahamoud militiamen would initiate a bloodbath, Hersi appointed an Isse Mahamoud supporter, Mohamed Haji Adan, to the made-up position of "deputy police commander," with instructions to bring Eyl under government control. On June 11, 2008, Haji travelled to Eyl with an escort of soldiers, leaving them on the outskirts of the town and sending an unarmed representative to demand a bribe from the pirates. The negotiations were brief; one of the pirate leaders asked Haji's man how much he wanted and sent him back with a shopping bag filled with $20,000 in cash. Haji promptly vacated his esteemed position and fled to the city of Galkayo, where he spent the following days and nights chewing khat. He was officially sacked four months later.[11]

Despite being far more capable than Hersi of cracking down on Eyl, according to Bryden, Farole has so far made no effort to impose central authority on his hometown, and has yet to even make a visit since his election. "The reason for him not doing so," Bryden wryly jibed, "is quite obvious."

Yet, according to Puntland government insiders, Farole has established new leadership in Eyl, including a mayor and a police commander equipped with a fleet of technicals (armed flatbed trucks). Since late 2009, Eyl had all but lost its status as a pirate base, with ships hijacked by Puntland gangs being taken to the more southern (and isolated) port of Garacad. Whether the pirate exodus was a result of Farole's leadership, or the general decline in the number of hijackings in the Gulf of Aden, is difficult to say for certain.

Bryden, for his part, was not convinced by the efforts of the Farole administration. "What's alarming," he said, "is how foreign governments have been duped into believing that Puntland is a real partner in anti-piracy, closing their eyes to the complicity."

Under mounting international pressure, said Bryden, there had been signs that Farole was starting to take the piracy issue more seriously—particularly since the US Treasury Department had placed Boyah and Garaad on a sanctions list in April 2010 (the US government, it appears, was not convinced by Boyah's quest for redemption). "Now that the US has designated Boyah and Garaad as wanted men," Bryden said, "he is in a position where he can no longer dodge the issue. If Farole wants good relations with the US, which by all accounts he does, he will need to get serious."

Indeed, Farole has made rapprochement with the international community—and in particular the United States—the cornerstone of his foreign policy. In July 2009, Farole accepted an invitation from the US State Department to appear before the House of Representatives Committee on Foreign Affairs. In his speech, Farole proposed a four-point counter-piracy plan to be financed with US money, which included the establishment of a coastal task force operating out of bases situated in eight towns along the Puntland coastline. So far, this plan has not materialized.[12]

The UN Monitoring Group's accusations elicited a predictably irate reaction from the Puntland government. In a press statement shortly after the release of the group's March 2010 report, President Farole hit back, attacking the credibility of the report's sources as well as Bryden himself. "The report's authors used sources that include politicians who are opportunists or are opposed to Puntland's self-development," he said. "Even some of the report's authors are politically motivated to discredit Puntland as a way of achieving another hidden goal."[13]

It was not the first accusation of anti-Puntland bias levelled against Bryden: in the past, he has openly campaigned for the international recognition of Somaliland—with which Puntland has a hostile relationship—indicating a political stance that made him an unusual choice to head up a UN body. The overtly pro-Somaliland independence reports he issued while director of the International Crisis Group's Africa Program in the mid-2000s earned him the enduring enmity of Puntland government, which responded by declaring him a *persona non grata*. This order was still standing as of 2010; the group's March report had been compiled without Bryden ever having set foot in Puntland.

*   *   *

Though the Puntland government, as Bryden suggested, has become increasingly willing to pursue the pirates on land, enthusiasm alone may not be sufficient to offset its lack of capacity. With an annual budget in the range of $20 million, derived almost exclusively from Bossaso port taxes, the Puntland government cannot afford an effective police force, let alone a justice system capable of processing hundreds of suspected pirates.

With such meagre resources at his disposal, Puntland's president can perhaps be better described as an inter-clan mediator than as the leader of a modern state. Even to fund basic state services, the president is routinely forced to beg for handouts from unconventional sources. Addressing an assembly of Bossaso businessmen at a dinner one evening, Farole appealed for donations to pay for a list of absurdly modest projects: replacing road signs, long ago stripped bare for the valuable metal; building a six-kilometre road from the livestock inspection station to the port; constructing a small hospital.

Given Puntland's capacities, the counter-piracy potential of the local military forces is limited. The Darawish's five to six thousand soldiers are garrisoned at Garowe, Bossaso, and Qardho—far from the locus of pirate activity—so any land operation against the pirates involves transporting troops hundreds of kilometres across roadless terrain. The logistical difficulties in deploying such a response make successful results extremely rare, and almost entirely dependent on timely local intelligence gathering.

One such operation occurred when I was with the president's entourage in Bossaso. Acting on a tip-off, Farole led an impromptu raid on the village of Marero, a well-known human trafficking and piracy launching site just east of Bossaso. In what was more a public relations exercise than a model for future action, Puntland security forces captured two speedboats, several outboard motors, barrels of fuel, food, and ladders. The seized equipment was proudly displayed to local media in lieu of the would-be pirates themselves, who had absconded in a speedboat as the troops approached.

If provided with sufficient financial and technical support from the international community aimed at overhauling its police and justice system, the Puntland government would be in a good position to tackle piracy on land. Like other kinds of undesirables who move and find shelter amongst civilians—militants, revolutionaries, even common criminals—the pirates' success depends on the goodwill and protection of the local people. Though initially welcomed as heroes, they have become increasingly unpopular amongst the local inhabitants due to their perceived un-Islamic influence.

It was perhaps with a view to mending community relations that Boyah's redemption movement had proved so popular amongst his former colleagues. Of these ex-pirates, perhaps none had expressed a greater desire to reform than Momman, a taciturn and thoughtful man whom I had first met at the khat picnics outside Garowe. Two weeks after the picnics, in July 2009, the two Omars procured me an invitation to visit Momman at his home.

8

Momman

MOMMAN'S HOUSE STOOD ALONE AMID A FIELD OF RUBBLE ON the outskirts of Garowe, past the ruins of the long-abandoned airport, a vast tract of stone and concrete slabs struggling to poke through decades of layered dust. Nearby was a Japanese-funded settlement for internally displaced persons, ramshackle rows of tent-like structures cast in cracking concrete and tin—a damning testament to what a million dollars buys with Somali contractors. The only human activity in the early afternoon heat was a lone woman labouring over a wash bucket with a few haggard, half-naked children scampering in orbits around her.

As with many upscale Somali dwellings, the wall ringing Momman's compound was a vibrant sky blue, decorated with brilliant yellow and red circles and triangles, like a child's finger painting. We parked outside the walls beside another 4x4; this area of town was so deserted that there was no serious risk of theft. We had come directly from the khat *suq*, where, as a friendly offering, I had financed the purchase of several hefty bags of the drug.

Momman had once been Boyah's running mate, a founding father of the core group of Eyl fishermen-cum-pirates, before he split off to form a group of his own. Judging by the size of his house, he had enjoyed a fair measure of success prior to joining the recent pirate redemption movement.

We moved through the gate and into a courtyard carved up by weeds and empty except for a lonely gazebo. My two Special Police Unit guards secured themselves a ration of khat and found a spot under the gazebo to settle down and chew. We were told to wait outside as Momman prepared the house for us.

After about five minutes we received permission to go inside. The dim hallway leading into the house hit my eyes as a formless smudge of black and blue as I left the bright sun of the courtyard behind. Following the Omars' example, I slipped off my sandals and stepped barefoot into a low-lit, spacious room serving as a joint dining and living space. The cloying smell of Arabian perfume hung heavily in the air, reminiscent of the scented tissues provided at Somali restaurants following a meal. To my immediate left a sleek stainless-steel fridge and freezer rested flush against the door jamb; further down the adjoining wall, a brand-new twenty-one-inch TV and DVD player shared a beige wall unit with neat stacks of china. At the room's midpoint it cast off its modernist airs and morphed into an approximation of a sultan's tent: a three-piece divan framed an ornate crimson carpet, itself encircled by thick crimson drapes that blocked the daylight struggling through the barred windows behind them. Reddish, gold-tasselled bolsters sat propped on the floor against the base of the divan, while a few smaller similarly coloured pillows were scattered on the cushions above.

This was one of the nicest houses I had yet seen in Somalia, and I paid Momman the compliment. He was quick to correct me. "This is not my house." he said. "It belongs to my wife and kids." I felt like a tax agent investigating the assets of a mafia don.

Colonel Omar, dressed in his usual striped tracksuit, stocking cap, and scarf, lay staring at the ceiling on the divan across from me. He cradled his AK across his chest, almost caressing it. He was still khat sober: fifty days and counting. On the ground, the smaller Omar reclined against the cushion propped beneath the Colonel's legs. To his left sat his driver, a blithe, lanky man named Mahad.

Momman settled at the head of the gathering, leaning on the

floor against a bolster. Behind his head on the divan lay a loaded Belgian semi-automatic pistol—the little brother, around these parts, to the AK-47. Momman was flanked on either side by two of his former foot soldiers, Mohamed and Abdirahman (not their real names), who casually lounged, fastidiously picking at khat stems.

Momman, like Boyah, looked to be in his early forties, with broad shoulders that gave him an air of great physical strength. But in place of Boyah's free-flowing goat's tuft and traditional elder's garb were a meticulously trimmed goatee and an equally dapper combo of striped red dress shirt and olive slacks. His face was hard, his eyes old and almost fatigued, their gaze producing the impression—impossible to feign—that he did not care at all what I thought of him. He studied me intently, his eyes tracking over my face, and I found it difficult to meet them. His rare smiles slipped by with obvious reluctance, as if his facial muscles had briefly triumphed over his brain for control of his expression.

His austere gaze remained unchanged even when I produced the copious bags of khat I had brought with me. We dropped the black plastic bags in the centre of the carpet and clustered around them, like children around a campfire, an atmosphere that was instantly dashed when Momman rose and threw open the drapes, flooding the room with daylight. I settled back against the cushions, letting my *ma'awis* cascade comfortably over my folded legs, and picked apart the binding of a bundle. Selecting a stalk, I stripped away the tough, leathery leaves until only the soft shoots remained. As I lifted it to my mouth, the hint of bitterness hitting my nostrils carried with it a vision of the day to come: the stomach pains, the nervous chain-smoking, the tossing and turning until the early hours of the morning. Time itself doesn't seem quite real when you're chewing khat; the activity is perfectly in tune with Somalia—the slow, lethargic chewing keeps pace with the plodding of the days, lives measured out in pulpy mouthfuls. "Khat days" are endless, and there was no rush to begin the interview. I relaxed and waited for tongues to loosen.

In the meantime, I produced my backgammon set and played a few games with my interpreter Omar. Mohamed and Abdirahman glanced over as we played and asked some idle questions, but before long Colonel Omar descended from his perch on the divan and snatched the board away from his cousin, pulling it close to him where the others were unable to see it. He pointed aggressively at my chest, indicating a challenge.

The Colonel's militaristic philosophy on life was nowhere better expressed than in his backgammon game. He hit checkers in a mad frenzy whenever it was possible to do so, bellowing in victory each time. I tried to explain through Omar why restraint was necessary, but my interpreter lacked the translational nuance to properly convey backgammon strategy. I did what I could, uttering the Somali word for "dangerous"—*khatar*—after each ill-advised move, but it was of little use. After each inevitable loss, the Colonel scowled and half-jokingly accused me of cheating, wagging his finger.

Ignoring our game, Momman remained fixated on the television set, which was showing the latest Somali Broadcasting Corporation footage of Mogadishu in flames, the result of yet another Al-Shabaab suicide bombing. The conversation somehow turned to the multiple foreign journalists who had been kidnapped in Puntland, some by their own guards. "Here, in the Nugaal valley, we don't kidnap people who are working with us," Momman said, smiling at me for the first time. "It's not our culture."

Someone produced a tall thermos containing the saccharine tea that traditionally accompanies khat to counteract its bitter taste, and I poured a small helping into a cup. Every so often, Momman's wife wandered into the room, arranging the already tidy chairs or checking the placement of the immaculately stowed chinaware.

Momman picked up his handgun and absently began to toy with it. Bored and anxious to develop some kind of rapport, I nonchalantly requested to see it. He removed the clip and passed it through an assembly line of hands until it reached me. I fiddled with the safety for a few seconds and examined the barrel, then cocked the hammer a few times for good measure, nodding approvingly.

An hour and a half on, heaps of discarded khat stalks joined ciga-
rette butts in mounting piles next to half-drained teacups. Attention
turned to the TV as a procession of images of Somalia's past leaders
began to scroll across the screen. Abdirahman and Mohamed excit-
edly named each one for me as his photo appeared. Momman sat in
silence, watching the television and chewing ponderously.

Enough time had passed for the khat to take effect, so I decided
to ask Momman some questions. The tale he began to recount was
by now familiar to my ears. "Boyah and I used to fish together," he
said. "At first, we operated together in the same group, but later we
split into different ones. There were a lot of independent groups .
. . around fifteen of them. We used to only go after illegal fishing
ships," he explained. It wasn't until 1999, according to Momman,
that Boyah attacked his first commercial ship. "We started attacking
them when we realized we couldn't fight against fishing ships anymore," owing to the improved state of their armament. "Commercial
ships go into our waters, and they don't pay any fees."

Momman's success soon elevated him, as with Boyah, to the
position of financier: "I was the one who bought everything for the
missions," he explained, sometimes for his own group, but also for
others. "We helped each other out."

Boyah had taken credit for hijacking dozens of ships, but when
asked for his own tally, Momman hesitated. "I can't tell you that," he
said, "it's a secret." He paused, musing. "I got a lot of good ones."

I decided to change tack. Boyah told me that his favourite ship
was the *Golden Nori*, I said, referring to the Japanese chemical
tanker he had steered into Bossaso port, What's yours? The attempt
met defeat against Momman's hard eyes.

"I don't want to talk about that," he answered. "I'm ashamed of
what I did."

I pressed further, desperate for any scraps of information he
could give me about the ships: the nationalities of the crew, their
cargos or destinations.

"No, I won't give you any of those details," Momman said, "because you'll be able to figure out the names of the ships later on."

"He's not stupid," Omar interjected.

Momman invariably hijacked any question aimed at illuminating his buccaneering past and steered it back to the topic of his redemption. "I want to have a good career, and not have it ruined by my past deeds," he said. "I want to be another man." He gave April 20 as marking the beginning of this new life, which he insisted was before the redemption movement had come into fashion. "I renounced piracy before the Sheikh [Abdulkhadar] started taking people to mosque and making them swear off piracy. I made the decision on my own.

"I know it's bad to be a pirate, but at least pirates never kill anyone," he said. "What warships do, especially the Indian ones, is really bad. When they run into a pirate boat, they will kill them, or take their food and fuel and abandon them until they eat one another." He added, in a disgusted tone, "It would be better to just kill them." Even in the international media, the Indian navy had earned a reputation for heavy-handedness; perhaps most infamous was the November 2008 incident in which the Indians blew a Thai fishing ship out of the water with all hands on board, later claiming they had mistaken it for a pirate mothership.

"The Americans, they are the nicest ones," Momman said. "The rest of them just want to do their job—they don't care who dies."

Momman's warm feelings towards the Americans had come from personal experience, like the time they responded to the SOS of a ship he had hijacked—the name of which Momman naturally refused to disclose. "About forty minutes after we boarded the ship, the Americans appeared and started shooting at us," he said. Like Boyah, Momman could recall with surprising accuracy the designations of the warships hemming him in: B135, B132, 125, 128. "The numbers kept changing" as ships arrived and retreated, he said.

"The Americans were talking at us through the ship's loudspeakers, but we just ignored them and moved the ship to Eyl. They were warning us to leave the ship within twenty-four hours, or they would attack," he said, smiling. "Twenty-four hours later, they repeated the same message."

Gunfire from the American ships raked the cliffs overlooking the beach at Eyl. "Then they shot at the fishing boats on the beach," said Momman, "because they thought they were going to bring us supplies. They fired near to the boats as they tried to approach us from shore. They stopped them from bringing us food." It was then, according to Momman, that the ship's owners requested that the Americans back off, paving the way for a painless ransom negotiation.

Reminded of these glory days, Momman began to speak more freely of his past life, sounding almost nostalgic. "We used to take a lot of dry food with us, extra sugar, a little flour. Enough for seven days. We would cook on board," he said.

"It was never that hard to climb up onto the deck—it depends on how high up the ship is, how fast it's going, but usually it's very easy. Personally, I've never seen the crew fighting back. Most people would go and lock themselves inside, some would come out with their hands out, saying, 'What do you guys want?'"

And was the crew ever afraid?

"Definitely, they would freak out. But we tried to calm them down, saying, 'We're not going to hurt you if you take our orders.' We would tell them, 'You'll be all right . . . we're not here to kill you.' We never had to kill anyone."

Momman lamented that things had gotten much more dangerous since those days. Many of his former colleagues had disappeared without a trace in recent times. "Some of my friends are still missing," he said. "About two months ago, some of them washed up dead on the coast, near Garacad," presumably either drowned or killed by the international naval forces. "The families of the missing boys are really upset about it; they don't know where they are or whether they're dead or alive," said Momman. "It's starting to create a lot of anger. Who knows what their families will do.

"Also, some of these young boys have gotten twenty years in

Bossaso jail," he said. "That angers their families too, but at least when they are in Somalia they can go visit them."

* * *

It is not only foreign navies that are responsible for dead Somalis in the surf, but possibly the pirates themselves. The stretch of the Gulf of Aden linking northern Somalia and Yemen is one of the world's busiest human smuggling routes; often when travelling from Garowe to Bossaso, I would see dozens of Oromo migrants alongside the road, staffs in hand, walking the hundreds of kilometres from the highlands of Ethiopia to Bossaso under the burning sun. Many I later observed camped in huddles outside the Bossaso compound of the UN High Commission for Refugees, but many others undoubtedly joined the thousands of Somalis making the risky dash for Yemen each year.

Tragically, those who smuggle them often do not complete the job, forcing migrants into the water kilometres from shore in order to avoid Yemeni coastal patrols; according to the UN's Mixed Migration Task Force, 1–7 per cent of those making the journey from 2007 to 2009 died in the attempt.[1] Pirate groups, other UN agencies have claimed, are directly involved in human trafficking. It makes sense: pirates already use Yemeni ports to obtain smuggled weapons, and pirate organizations could use their equipment and smuggling networks to achieve a perverse economy of scale by bridging the piracy and human smuggling "industries."

Momman agreed, but made it clear that his generation had never been involved in such activities. "The pirates operating now are definitely doing that," he said, "but it wasn't going on earlier." According to him, the going rate for a trip to Yemen was $200 for a spot in a "small boat"—holding about thirty people—and $100 for a place in a more crowded "big boat"—one carrying eighty to a hundred people. The business had a dual purpose that went beyond the money: the pirates, said Momman, used the migrants as a cover to conceal their activities from both the Puntland government and international naval forces. Unlike piracy, transporting people is not a crime, at least until an attempt is made to enter a foreign state illegally.

"They don't want the government to see that they are pirates," he explained. "They drop off [the migrants] and then go about their pirating." The idea was not completely far-fetched. During President Farole's impromptu raid on pirates in the village of Marero, his soldiers captured documents conclusively linking the gang to human smuggling.

Whether pirate gangs are amongst the many smuggling groups guilty of murdering their charges is unknown. But Momman doubted it: "They always deliver the people on time."

* * *

The desire to trace the poorly marked money trail always led my interviews to one central question: How do pirates spend their cash? Judging from Momman's response, it was the wrong question to ask.

"I told you before," he said, "this house is not mine, it's my wife's. I never used any piracy money to live on—it's *haram* to do so. We used that money to fund new pirate operations and to buy weapons. That's all. We don't build houses with it." Indeed, the like-minded devotion by other pirate headmen to continual capital reinvestment had allowed piracy to develop into a self-sustaining industry.

The fleeting Somali dusk had come and gone, and the strips of sky poking through the bars of the windows were now a deep navy blue. Colonel Omar roused himself from the couch and headed off to meet some visiting Kenyan documentary makers being hosted by the Farole family. The hours of continual chewing had taken their toll on me: gut rot was gnawing at my stomach lining and an indefinable pain was pounding my brain, but my body was taut with nervous energy, my jaw clenched. Omar and I were also scheduled to meet with the Colonel's Kenyan journalists, and his phone chimed every few minutes with the Colonel's insistent reminders. After about the seventh call within a quarter hour, I decided that the interview had reached its natural conclusion.

I picked up my half-finished bundle of khat and tossed it gently into Momman's dwindling pile. He protested; take it, please, I said, and he accepted.

Throughout the interview, Mohamed and Abdirahman had been content to let Momman act as their mouthpiece, perhaps because their own mouths had been too jammed with khat leaves to be of any service to them. As I was about to leave, Mohamed, who up until now had been fairly reticent, timidly requested permission to ask me a question: What, he hesitantly inquired, do people in the West think about pirates? "They think about people with eye patches," I replied, wondering in what mangled form my meaning would reach Mohamed's brain. The romantic stereotype of the swashbuckling pirate was so foreign to the Somalis' self-image that my many previous attempts to convey it had been met only with bemused glances.

As I got up to depart, blood rushing into my numbed legs, I asked permission to take a photo of Momman and his two colleagues. *Maya*, no, he said, waving away my camera. I reminded him that I had videotaped Momman, Boyah, and the other pirates during our recent khat picnic together. "I couldn't do anything about that," he answered. "Here, I can."

Memory would have to suffice. My last image of Momman, as his wife led us out the door, was of him reclining against a bolster, teacup in one hand, khat stalk in the other, staring pensively into the carpet.

9

The Policemen of the Sea

MOMMAN'S ANIMOSITY TOWARDS THE INTERNATIONAL NAVAL coalitions policing Somali waters was shared by many of his peers. Boyah, for one, still spoke with anger about the six men he lost, plucked into the sky by French navy helicopters and transported half a world away to face eventual trial in a Parisian courthouse. Yet he was quick to express his contempt for the international naval forces. "Sometimes, we capture vessels when warships are right around us," Boyah had told me during our first meeting. "We don't care about them. They're not going to stop us."

Though it is tempting to write off Boyah's remarks as empty bluster, the facts are harder to dismiss: the deployment of three multinational naval task forces beginning in late 2008 has done little to halt pirate attacks. Conversely, from 2008 to 2010 the number of hijackings continued to rise, and the trend had not abated as this book went to press.

When the Somali pirates exploded onto the scene following the end of the summer monsoon season in 2008, the world was caught unprepared. The only naval presence in the region was Combined Task Force 150 (CTF-150), a multinational coalition built around the US Fifth Fleet whose primary function was counter-terrorism. Following the sharp increase in the pirate threat, counter-piracy was hastily tacked onto CTF-150's mandate, though clearly only as a stopgap solution.

In October 2008, NATO finally announced plans to deploy a seven-warship task force by the year's end. Two months later, the European Union added its own flotilla to Somalia's increasingly congested waterways, EU Naval Force Somalia (EUNAVFOR, also designated "Atalanta"). And in January 2009, the United States proclaimed the creation of Combined Task Force 151 (CTF-151), a multinational fleet tasked with taking over counter-piracy operations from CTF-150. Independently operating navies from countries as diverse as China, India, Iran, Russia, and Malaysia also joined the fray, with the clear priority of defending their own nationals and flag vessels. As individual warships have come and gone at the behest of their home governments, the combined strength of the international coalition has varied between twenty-five and forty vessels, at an estimated annual cost of $1–$1.5 billion.

For many countries, the piracy crisis provided an ideal opportunity to flex naval muscles: Operation Atalanta was the very first maritime mission under the EU flag, China's deployment of three warships was its first overseas mission since 1949, and Germany's and Japan's respective contributions to Atalanta and CTF-151 exemplified the two nations' gradual movement away from five decades of dogmatic pacifism. The Somali pirates seemed to be an enemy that the whole world could agree on.

Yet these three fleets, the collective product of an unprecedented level of international naval cooperation, have been unable to stop a motley assortment of half-starved brigands armed with aging assault rifles and the odd grenade launcher. Many find it incomprehensible that, despite bristling with state-of-the-art weaponry and detection systems, Western warships have allowed the pirates to continue to hijack ships with seeming impunity.

Such an attitude fails to appreciate the sheer size of the area that international forces must cover. From the time the crew of a targeted vessel spots the oncoming hijackers and sends out a distress call, a nearby warship generally has a window of fifteen to forty minutes in which to respond before the pirates manage to board the vessel.

Assuming the ship is outfitted with a helicopter (which has a maximum speed of about 320 kilometres per hour) ready for immediate launch, it must be within about eighty kilometres of the scene of attack in order to have a realistic shot at mounting a successful rescue operation. Yet Somali pirate attacks have occurred along an east–west axis 3,000 kilometres wide, from the depths of the Indian Ocean to the Red Sea, and along a north–south axis ranging the 3,700 kilometres from Oman to Madagascar—an ocean surface area four-fifths the size of the United States. For the crews of the warships in the combined international naval effort, struggling to contain an estimated 1,500–2,000 pirates operating in small groups of six to twelve, hunting pirates must seem like playing a losing game of Whac-a-Mole. In fairness, controlling such a vast area is not quite as hopeless as I have made it out to be; pirate attacks tend to cluster around shipping lanes, and by patrolling these routes warships greatly improve their odds of disrupting pirate operations. But it is generally accepted that no purely military solution exists to the problem of Somali piracy—at least none that is both economically and politically feasible.

* * *

When EUNAVFOR warships sailed into the Gulf of Aden in December 2008, they came with a plan. In cooperation with the other naval forces, NAVFOR established the Internationally Recommended Transit Corridor (IRTC), a heavily patrolled safe zone running 650 kilometres along the Yemeni side of the Gulf of Aden. In conjunction with regularly scheduled convoy escorts, the IRTC was immediately effective in restoring some order to the stretch of water that wary mariners had nicknamed "Pirate Alley." But though the statistics show that the IRTC was initially effective in reducing the success rate of pirate attacks, the absolute number of hijackings steadily rose. In 2008, there were 134 attacks, mostly concentrated in the Gulf of Aden, resulting in 49 documented hijackings. In 2009, the number of attacks increased to 228, with 68 successful hijackings.

The next year saw 74 hijackings for 243 attacks, and as of February the figures for 2011 stood at 14 hijackings for 40 attacks—on pace to exceed the 2010 total.[1]

These numbers reveal a small drop in the hijacking success rate (37 per cent to 30 per cent) from 2008 to 2009,[2] corresponding to the increased naval presence towards the end of 2008 and the creation of the IRTC. Though the hijacking success rate has remained between 30 and 35 per cent since 2009, the economic incentive—as measured by ransom amounts—has been steadily increasing. In 2008, the average pirate ransom fell in the range of $1.25–$1.5 million, which grew to $2–$2.5 million in 2009 and to $3–$4 million in 2010, highlighted by the then record $9.5 million bounty paid to release MV *Samho Dream*, a South Korean oil tanker commandeered in April (the vessel earned her hijackers more than three times the amount garnered by the headline-grabbing supertanker *Sirius Star* merely a year earlier.) In 2008, the pirates earned a total of $25–$35 million, a figure that shot up to $70–$90 million the following year. Yet in 2010, as average ransoms spiralled upwards, ransom revenues surprisingly fell slightly, to $65–$85 million. With the number of hijackings continuing to rise, this seemingly paradoxical drop in earnings was explained by lengthening periods of captivity, as avaricious pirate bosses began to drag out negotiations for months longer in the hope of securing themselves premium ransoms. As a consequence, the majority of vessels hijacked in 2010 were not ransomed until well into 2011.

Of course, not every hijacked ship is a multi-million-dollar lottery ticket; many are dhows or small fishing trawlers manned by poor Yemeni or South Asian crews. Lacking the defence of being worth ransoming, the fishermen are often set adrift or even killed, their vessels converted for use as pirate motherships. Beginning in 2009, the proportion of fishing dhows as a percentage of total hijackings increased, probably to meet the soaring demand for motherships required by the pirates' Indian Ocean expansion. Exactly how many poor fishermen have fallen victim to Somali pirates will likely never be known; often neglected or abandoned by their parent companies, attacks against fishing vessels frequently go unreported to the International Maritime Bureau or other authorities. The untold brunt of brutality borne by Yemeni fishermen has prompted Puntland expert Stig Hansen to call these attacks "the hidden tragedy of piracy."[3]

*   *   *

Unlike rival street gangs, pirate groups do not have formally demarcated "turfs" that they jealously guard from their enemies. Yet the geographical locations of hijackings have correlated with remarkable accuracy to the geographical origins of the hijackers. All ships known to have been seized in the Gulf of Aden, for instance, have ended up in Puntland ports, while the vast majority of those hijacked in the far south, near the Seychelles and Madagascar, have been taken to Harardheere. Thus, as the choice pirate hunting ground shifted from the Gulf of Aden to the Indian Ocean, Puntland's strategic importance waned. Many pirate groups continued to operate out of the region, but they mostly used the southern port of Garacad, which had the dual advantages of being more remote and isolated than Eyl, as well as closer to the Indian Ocean shipping lanes.

Perversely, the constant naval pressure may also have bred a higher class of pirate, because the groups operating upwards of 1,500 kilometres into the Indian Ocean required a much higher level of sophistication—in terms of boats, supply logistics, navigational skills and equipment, and perhaps intelligence networks—than those who had previously floated in the Gulf of Aden, waiting for any target of opportunity to come along. The forces of artificial selection meant that only the most advanced pirate gangs were likely to survive in the new reality created by the Gulf of Aden safety corridor.

The pirates' Indian Ocean expansion did not go unnoticed by the international naval forces. In April 2010 I spoke to Commander John Harbour, the media spokesman for EUNAVFOR, via telephone from his London office. According to Harbour, the upper echelons of

EU leadership had vigorously debated how to respond to the pirates' change in tactics. Some voices, he said, had argued for a complete blockade of pirate ports along the entire length of the Somali coast, an approach that he viewed as unrealistic: "The Somali coast is over a thousand miles long, and although it's got maybe six or seven main [pirate] ports, we haven't even got enough ships to cover those. What we can do, with good intelligence, is find the pirate camps and sit off of them. These camps can be anything from a mothership, a couple of skiffs, and a few barrels on the shore covered by a tarpaulin, to ten motherships and thirty skiffs."

Locating and blockading these floating bases, often through information gathered by maritime patrol aircraft, formed the first pillar of the EU's latest counter-piracy strategy; by interdicting suspicious craft before they reached the international shipping lanes, NAVFOR hoped to contain the problem at its source. In many ways, NAVFOR's vessels had begun to operate like the defensive line of a football team, concentrating their forces at the line of scrimmage but positioning safeties further afield to intercept any opponent slipping through the perimeter. "The new strategy was basically to take the fight to the pirates," Harbour explained. "First, interdict them off their bases. Then, have ships available in a second layer, maybe one to two hundred miles off the coast, who can respond to attacks. Finally, have maritime patrol aircraft and ships in the deeper Indian Ocean, who can visit the scene after an attack has occurred."

Over the previous month, he estimated, NAVFOR had disrupted twenty-five pirate "attack groups"—each consisting of a mothership towing two skiffs—half of which had been intercepted before reaching open ocean, and half captured in the wake of attempted hijackings. The success of their shift in strategy, said Harbour, had provoked yet another tactical adaptation by the pirates. "They've discovered that we're sitting off the shore," he said, "so therefore they've started to throw their skiffs behind their 4x4s and go find a bit of deserted beach where they can launch the operation. We've also seen far more launches done from southern Somalia."